BRITAIN'S BEST POLITICAL CARTOONS 2020

Dr Tim Benson is Britain's leading authority on political cartoons. He runs the Political Cartoon Gallery and Café which is located near the River Thames in Putney. He has produced numerous books on the history of cartoons, including *David Low Censored*, *Giles's War*, *Churchill in Caricature*, *Low and the Dictators*, *The Cartoon Century: Modern Britain through the Eyes of Its Cartoonists*, *Drawing the Curtain: The Cold War in Cartoons*, *Over the Top: A Cartoon History of Australia at War* and *How to be British: A Cartoon Celebration*.

BRITAIN'S BEST POLITICAL CARTOONS 2020

Edited by Tim Benson

HUTCHINSON
LONDON

For Bobbie and Desiree Benson

1 3 5 7 9 10 8 6 4 2

Hutchinson
20 Vauxhall Bridge Road
London SW1V 2SA

Hutchinson is part of the Penguin Random House
group of companies whose addresses can be found
at global.penguinrandomhouse.com.

First published in the United Kingdom by Hutchinson in 2020

www.penguin.co.uk

A CIP catalogue record for this book is available from the British Library.

ISBN 9781786332509

Typeset in 11/15.5 pt Amasis MT Light by Jouve (UK), Milton Keynes

Printed and bound by L.E.G.O. SpA

Penguin Random House is committed to a sustainable future
for our business, our readers and our planet. This book is made from
Forest Stewardship Council® certified paper.

INTRODUCTION

Enoch **Powell once** said that all political careers end in failure. Might this be a dictum that also applies to political cartoonists? Many of these caricaturists, whether by choice or of necessity, continue with their work well past the age when most people swap professional life for gardening and Mediterranean cruises, but do they risk their reputation as a result?

It is an unusual state of affairs. In most professions, people look forward to reaching retirement so that they can leave behind the stress and drudgery of their working lives. But cartoonists, with the odd exception, generally prefer to carry on indefinitely – regardless of the deterioration in eyesight that comes with growing older. Even today, the majority of Britain's leading cartooning lights are in their 60s and 70s, with a minority of arriviste whippersnappers in their 30s and 40s.

Why is this the case? For many cartoonists, the answer is fear of missing out – the terrifying prospect of sitting bored at home with your feet up, when you could be helping to shape world news. 'I do not think it is an option,' says *The Times*'s Chris Duggan when asked about retirement. 'Daytime television? Stone-coloured windcheaters? Trips to the garden centre every week? Permanent lockdown? Not while there are such top satirists to illustrate, like Donald Trump, Boris Johnson and his éminence grise. Without cartoonists doing what they do, people might think they were serious!' When I asked Steve Bell if he had had any thoughts about retirement – suggesting he might want to swap his pens and inks for the occasional round of golf – he retorted, 'Who would want to play fucking golf? I hate fucking golf!' Stan McMurtry, known by his pen name 'Mac', very reluctantly retired in 2018 at the grand old age of 82. But he recently confessed that he desperately missed his drawing board, finding it difficult to be unable to comment on last year's general election as well as the machinations over Brexit.

'Oh, come on, Mac! You're supposed to walk happily into the sunset.'

The final cartoon Stan 'Mac' McMurty drew for the *Daily Mail*. He reluctantly retired in 2018 after 50 years working for the newspaper.

Many cartoonists emphasise that cartooning is still a source of great pleasure. Drawing is much more than just a job – it is a calling. To these individuals, the simple enjoyment of creating political cartoons is everything. Peter Brookes, for example, says he finds the exhilaration of being involved in the editor's early-morning press briefings at *The Times* immeasurable. Steve Bell also points to the joy that comes from creating satire, saying nothing interests him in the way that cartooning does (and that he is no good at anything else). He still relishes the daily challenge of testing his wits by coming up with beautiful compositions. 'It's excruciating at times, trying to work out what am I going to do today,' he says, '[but] I get a massive buzz from solving, what is, to all intents and purposes, a puzzle.' Bell says he could 'drop off the perch' at any moment – but insists he will only retire when he stops enjoying cartooning.

Peter Schrank has gone so far as to say that, once you get a taste of the excitement of creating a daily cartoon, it is almost impossible to give it up. 'Every cartoon is a gamble,' Schrank comments. 'Will you come up with an idea in time? Is it any good? Will you be able to draw it fast enough and will it work when finished? At the end of each working day you have a result, for better or worse . . . It's an addiction, like gambling, or an adrenalin fix. Being engaged with events, being part of the political discourse in however small a way, remains very rewarding.' Political cartooning, once under your skin, is difficult to retire from.

And that's not to mention the money. Cartooning is a precarious profession, and many cartoonists don't have much in the way of retirement savings. As Bell puts it, 'Most cartoonists are freelance and we all have no choice but to carry on working. I couldn't live on my pension, so retirement is not an option.' Patrick

Peter Brookes pokes gentle fun at Theresa May, whose beleaguered government was on its last legs when this cartoon was drawn in January 2019. It was published days after Andy Murray announced his retirement from tennis.

Blower, a cartoonist for the *Daily Telegraph*, agrees. 'Once you've reached the top, there's nowhere else to go; no cosy sinecures, no university chairs, no well-remunerated non-executive directorships, no memoirs that anyone would buy, no diversification into books, no TV punditry,' he says. 'We're just misfits tagging on to the arse end of newspapers. The choice is: cartoons or oblivion.'

Besides, many cartoonists fear that if they do stand down, there is no way back should they change their minds. When boxers retire, they often miss the adrenalin of the fight and come to regret their decision to stop – leading to the time-honoured tradition of the disastrous boxer's comeback. For cartoonists there is no room for such comebacks: the competition is fierce and opportunities for re-employment are slim. And this induces many cartoonists to continue well into their third acts; there have only ever been a handful of full-time cartooning positions, and the lucky incumbents tend to cling on to them for decades.

Indeed, the annals of cartoon history are littered with immediately regretted retirements on the part of cartoonists. In 1969, Leslie Illingworth of the *Daily Mail* and *Punch* retired to live in France. But by 1973, short of money and under fire from the taxman for unpaid back taxes, he leapt at the chance to stand in for the Australian Paul Rigby on the *Sun* for a month. Upon his return, Rigby felt sorry for Illingworth's plight and decided to give up his regular weekly cartoon for the *News of the World*, so Illingworth could take over. However, in June 1976, Illingworth suffered a stroke. Recounting that his 'brain had gone', he stood down as a cartoonist. The only happy retirement story I know of comes from John Musgrave-Wood, also of the *Mail*, better known by his pseudonym Emmwood. In August 1975, he decided he was bored with 'politics, senior personnel and editors who thought that they, being whizz kids, knew more about cartooning than cartoonists with forty years' experience'. He retired to Provence to concentrate all his efforts on painting.

Alas, Emmwood's tale is hardly representative. These days, finding employment as a political cartoonist is often described as filling dead men's shoes. Peter Brookes has mentioned to me on numerous occasions that Morten Morland is waiting for him to die so that he can replace him as *The Times*'s leading cartoonist. The result is that cartooning in Britain remains dominated by 'grumpy old men' who hang on until they are fired or carried out feet-first.

You might think that the grumpy-old-men syndrome afflicting British cartooning is a recent development. But you'd be wrong. There's a long and venerable tradition of cartoonists carrying on working through aging, illness and right up to death.

Usually the first thing to go is a cartoonist's eyesight. When the 81-year-old caricaturist and cartoonist Wally Fawkes noticed, after an unbroken 62-year career, that his eyesight had suddenly started to seriously deteriorate, he felt there was no alternative but to call it a day. He could no longer capture a likeness, which is, of course, vital when it comes to caricature. According to Fawkes, 'Every time I drew someone, when I took a closer look, it didn't look right at all.' However, unlike most of his cartooning colleagues, he at least had a major interest to fall back on, that of being a jazz musician. 'I think I would be a bit sadder about the whole business if I did not have the clarinet playing,' he said. Remarkably, two of the greatest cartoonists in history – *Punch*'s Sir John Tenniel and the *Express*'s Carl Giles – both had major problems with their eyesight from an early age. They were each partially blinded at the very start of their careers, at the age of 20. Tenniel lost sight in his right eye after being caught by his father's foil whilst fencing, and Giles was involved in a serious motorcycle accident that left him blind in one eye and deaf in one ear. Yet they were undeterred by the loss of sight, which did not stop them from producing incredibly detailed compositions. In the end, however, the constant strain on their one good eye meant that the quality of their drawings suffered. Both were forced to retire, Tenniel at 80 and Giles at 75.

In the glory days of twentieth-century cartooning, however, the health risks of being a cartoonist went well beyond fading vision. In the past, just about every cartoonist chain-smoked. Looking through old black and white photographs of political cartoonists, you rarely see them without a

Carl Giles at his drawing board in his studio, 9 February 1991. Towards the end of his career Giles's eyesight was fading so he used a magnifying glass to see his work.

cigarette, cigar or pipe in hand. And so many cartoonists fell victim to tobacco. Carl Giles' health issues were exacerbated by poor circulation, brought on by a lifetime of chain-smoking, which led to the amputation of both his legs shortly before he retired. Sidney Strube of the *Express*, another lifelong smoker, died at 65. David Low – arguably the twentieth century's best cartoonist – developed emphysema from smoking, which greatly affected his ability to use his brush precisely. As the illness worsened, there was a tangible decline in his draughtsmanship.

It became apparent to the *Guardian*, Low's employer since 1953, that the great man was on the wane. But they could not bring themselves to fire the most famous cartoonist of them all. Low drew his last cartoon for the *Guardian* on 30 April 1963. The following day he was hospitalised. Less than five months later he was dead.

Low is one of many cartoonists who doggedly continued on despite health issues. Leading figures such as Linley Sambourne, Will Dyson, Raymond 'JAK' Jackson and Michael Cummings all died from heart attacks at their drawing boards. In 1981, Charles Schulz, creator of *Peanuts* and the wealthiest cartoonist in the world, refused to retire even after undergoing quadruple-bypass surgery. In spite of a hand tremor and a diagnosis of colon cancer, he steadfastly refused to give up drawing his daily strip. On 12 February 2000, the night before his final *Peanuts* cartoon was published, Schulz died in his sleep. Other cartoonists were simply cut off mid-flow. In 1945, Sir Bernard Partridge climbed up Big Ben to paint the London skyline. The 84-year-old lost his balance, slipped and fell to the ground. Miraculously, he survived

A gathering of political cartoonists in 1942 showing Carl Giles, David Low, Sidney Strube, Leslie Illingworth and Victor Weisz 'Vicky', most with a pipe or cigarette in their mouth.

the fall – only to be run over and killed by the ambulance that was sent to rescue him.

Apart from the risk of working yourself to death, there is also the risk of working yourself to obsolescence. Any cartoonist who stays on the job too long is at risk of producing work that is dated, repetitive or out of touch. Well before his Big Ben misadventure, Bernard Partridge had long since outstayed his welcome at *Punch*; by the time he died, his overdrawn, pompous and curiously lifeless style had been outdated for decades. He was described by one critic as 'a veritable coelacanth among cartoonists – his ornate sesquipedalian style an ossified relic of a bygone age'. As Partridge's health declined, Leslie Illingworth was often invited to fill in for him – much to the older man's annoyance. Partridge expected to be treated with extreme deference, having been at *Punch* since 1891; indeed, Illingworth recalled being bundled down the back stairs whenever Partridge came into the building. In time, Illingworth would become the Grand Old Man of cartooning himself. As he approached the end of his own career in the 1960s and 1970s, Illingworth would say that he had managed to survive so long because 'when the editor comes in looking for someone to sack, I hide behind the door and he doesn't see me'.

It is not just a cartoonist's aesthetic that can

THE WEREWOLVES

"Of course it's rather hard to do the goose-step like this."

Bernard Partridge's penultimate cartoon for *Punch*. Published in April 1945, the cartoon ridicules Adolf Hitler and Heinrich Himmler for their so-called 'Werewolf' plan, a network of Nazi resisters to the Allied invasion.

perhaps inevitably, become old-fashioned. The acerbic post-war cartoonist Michael Cummings, for example, was ultimately let go from the *Express* in 1993 because his editor considered him to be 'too dated'. Cummings did admit to being out of step; he deplored the development of new forms of satire like ITV's *Spitting Image*, which seemed to him 'tasteless, sickly and sadistic'. *Guardian* columnist Edward Pearce believed that Les Gibbard was also let go because he had become out of step with the times. 'Gibbard was out because of a regressive fashion. "Back to Gillray," ' Pearce remarked. Gibbard's style was gentler and politer than that of either Bell or the visceral Rowson, and in his cartoons there was 'not a pile of excrement in sight'. It is a problem that has afflicted more recent cartoonists, too. Michael Heath, aged 85, still regularly draws cartoons for the *Mail on Sunday*, although his critics say that he is still drawing in the same way he did in the 1960s and, as a result, his work feels dated. By the time Stan McMurtry left the *Mail* in 2018, many of his visual references harked back to the twentieth century: British soldiers in 1950s National Service uniforms, and City workers wearing bowler hats and sock suspenders. As the cartoonist Peter Schrank puts it, 'It's OK to refer to our shared cultural heritage, but you also have to remain aware of what interests

become dated, however. Many great cartoonists have found that they can't keep up with the zeitgeist – their cultural references and humour,

younger generations. If you think film history ended with the Connery James Bond, it's time to quit.'

Once a cartoonist's talent begins to wane, they can rapidly become their editor's bête noire. Take the story of Sidney Strube. The most popular cartoonist of the interwar period and the highest-paid man in Fleet Street, Strube was adored by the millions who followed him in the *Daily Express* – which then had the largest circulation of any national newspaper in the world. But even he had his day. Three and a half decades after he joined, Strube was fired in December 1947 because, according to cartoonist Michael Cummings, he had become 'too repetitive and stale'. To make matters worse, he was fired on his birthday. In a memo to Lord Beaverbrook, the owner of the paper, the *Express*'s chief executive explained the decision to sack Strube. Attributing the decision to a number of recent 'very indifferent Strube cartoons', the memo describes the effect the decision had on the great man: 'After 36 years on the paper our decision obviously came as great shock. His attitude was a mixture of incoherence and a great belief in himself.' According to the note, Strube couldn't comprehend 'how anyone could decide to drop a great artist like himself and continue with a poor one like Giles.'

Even the great David Low was once forced to leave a newspaper – in his case the *Evening Standard*, which he had joined in 1927. Despite Low's genius in skewering Hitler and Mussolini, as the 1940s wore on, his editor, Herbert Gunn, came to feel that Low's talents were dwindling. And he wasn't alone. The *Evening Star* cartoonist Frederick Joss wrote in July 1949, 'I have heard people ask: "What's happened to Low?" . . . Low always held that cartoonists need not be funny. But he used to be very funny himself. His occasional sermons were

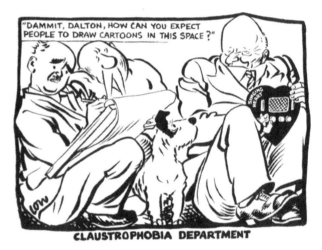

David Low created this cartoon on 22 July 1947 after his editor at the *Evening Standard* repeatedly reduced the space allotted for his work, ultimately forcing him to leave the paper. The cartoon features Hugh Dalton who, as chancellor of the Exchequer from 1945 to 1947, oversaw the policy of paper rationing which dramatically restricted the size of post-war newspapers.

outweighed by his gags and jabs. The gags have all but disappeared. The sermons have remained.'

In Low's case, though, his reputation made him effectively unsackable – Lord Beaverbrook described him as 'the man he couldn't fire' – and so Gunn adopted an underhand tactic. Even though Low's contract stipulated that his cartoons should be given a half-page, Gunn repeatedly shrank the space allotted to him. This was a blow: in the words of Michael Cummings, 'a cartoonist always knows when he is no longer wanted when they start shrinking the space available for his cartoons'. In a letter to Gunn, Low explained the effect of this war of attrition: 'The new size will permit only the bare illustration of ideas and will make artistic quality not merely difficult but impossible. This is a dismal prospect for me, who wants to DRAW, and my reputation, which must suffer a decline here and wherever *Evening Standard* syndications go.' The row no doubt contributed to Low's decision to leave the publication for the *Daily Herald* in 1950.

Another way editors force out cartoonists is even sneakier: gradually reducing their weekly commissions. When Lord Winterton was editor of *The World* between 1910 and 1911 he did exactly this to avoid humiliating Leslie Ward, the famous caricaturist known as 'Spy'. '[He] was getting on in

An Andy Davey cartoon for the *Sun* in 2010, responding to the news that it would be made illegal for employers to fire staff when they reached 65 because of their age.

years even at that time, and his work was not quite what it had been earlier,' Winterton would explain to Sidney Strube decades later. 'As I thought the public were getting a little bit tired of it, I arranged that he should alternate each week with "Sem", and though the old man resented this at first, he eventually agreed to this course.'

Today's cartoonists are, if anything, even more likely to be forced into retirement. With circulations and revenues dwindling, few newspaper editors are willing to keep cartoonists on out of largesse. And in recent years several of Britain's most venerable cartoonists have come under pressure to leave their roles.

To name a few: Rick Brookes, who took over from Carl Giles at the *Daily Express,* resigned from the *Metro* in November 2011 at the age of 63, and has never worked for a national newspaper since. Following five decades at the *Sunday Times*, Gerald Scarfe was fired from that newspaper in 2017 at the age of 81; after a short spell at the *Evening Standard*, he also left that newspaper in 2019. David Gaskill resigned from the *Sun* in 2011 at the age of 72 after a dispute with management; he claimed, 'They proved very difficult to work for, and the number of ideas I submitted went through the roof, resulting in my finally walking out. I just couldn't handle it any more. Not a good career move as it would turn out.' He also never worked as a full time cartoonist again. And, of course, Stan McMurtry drew his last cartoon for the *Daily Mail* at the end of 2018.

But such anecdotes can only tell part of the story. For every Scarfe, there is a Steve Bell – who shows no sign of slowing down as he approaches his eighth decade (even though, as he puts it, his eyesight 'ain't what it used to be'). For every McMurtry, there is a Peter Brookes – 77 at the time of writing – and still producing several cartoons a week for *The Times*. And with age comes great experience. Although Brookes admits to finding the process of cartooning more tiring than he once did, he says his age is an asset. The older you are, 'the more tricks you've got up your sleeve to get an idea across', he says. Indeed, with age his judgement has arguably become even sharper. 'If, as I edge towards 80, I can still feel no qualms at ripping up a cartoon I'd been lovingly working on because a juicier political news story had just broken, then maybe what I do is a vocation,' Brookes remarks. 'The moment I feel "Oh, that'll do" is the moment I'll chuck it in.' He adds, 'I have no plans to retire. They'll have to carry me out.'

The satirical connoisseur can take heart from the UK's vibrant cartooning culture, which will surely survive the retirement of even our greatest cartoonists. When coronavirus hit our shores in early 2020, it wasn't just established satirists who rose to the challenge of sketching our greatest political crisis in decades. These pages contain the work of four generations of cartoonists, from septuagenarians to millennials. It is another reminder that the future of the form is in safe hands.

THE CARTOONS

September saw the arrival of Dilyn, Boris Johnson's and Carrie Symonds' new dog. A few days before Dilyn's arrival, the prime minister had announced the suspension of Parliament to prevent MPs frustrating his Brexit legislation. Johnson's statement outside 10 Downing Street had been drowned out by protestors chanting 'stop the coup'. Some commentators suggested that Dilyn, a rescue pup with a misaligned jaw, may have been introduced by government aides to soften Johnson's public image. Brookes comments, 'This is how I prefer to do [Cummings] now, rather evil-looking, Svengali-like, and scruffy with his signature quilted jacket. Here he is carrying Boris the dog inside, which I think sums up their relationship pretty well.'

4 September 2019
Peter Brookes
The Times

21 Conservative rebels, including former cabinet ministers Philip Hammond, David Gauke, Rory Stewart and Ken Clarke, had the Tory whip removed after voting with opposition parties to prevent a no-deal Brexit. Also amongst them was Sir Nicholas Soames, Winston Churchill's grandson, who commented that he had only 'voted against the Conservative Party three times in 37 years'. The House of Commons voted 328 to 301 to take control of the agenda and delay the UK's exit date, thereby quashing the possibility of a no-deal Brexit in October.

5 September 2019
Seamus Jennings
Independent

6 September 2019
Nicola Jennings
Guardian

Around the same time that he was expelling Tory rebels, the prime minister had to contend with the resignation of his brother, Jo Johnson, MP for Orpington. Jo said that he had been torn by an 'unresolvable tension' between 'family loyalty and the national interest'. Boris Johnson, who had pronounced that he would rather 'die in a ditch' than delay Brexit, said of his brother's departure, 'Look, people disagree about the EU. The way to unite the country, I'm afraid, is to get this thing done.'

with apologies to Goya Ingram Pinn

THE SLEEP OF REASON PRODUCES MONSTERS

Green Party MP Caroline Lucas accused Jacob Rees-Mogg of being 'contemptuous of this house and of the people' after he was seen reclining on the front bench of the House of Commons while MPs debated the UK's future outside of the EU. Labour's Anna Turley labelled Rees-Mogg the 'physical embodiment of arrogance, entitlement, disrespect and contempt for our Parliament'. When asked whether he thought his repose had been wise, Rees-Mogg replied, 'In hindsight, I think not.'

7 September 2019
Ingram Pinn
Financial Times

FIRED...

IT'S WHAT HE WOULD HAVE WANTED!

12 September 2019
Dave Brown
Independent

In a series of tweets, Donald Trump sacked his national security advisor, John Bolton, saying that he 'disagreed strongly' with his top aide. The firing appeared to surprise White House officials, who an hour earlier had announced Bolton's appearance alongside government ministers at a press conference. Shortly after the announcement, Bolton texted a Fox News presenter who was live on-air, saying 'I resigned, having offered to do so last night.'

'The divisions between Corbyn and Watson over Brexit were making headlines, which gave me the opportunity to use, "Elementary, my dear Watson," which is what I really wanted to do,' the cartoonist comments. Labour's deputy leader Tom Watson had put forward his argument that the party should 'unequivocally back Remain' in a second Brexit referendum. Jeremy Corbyn said he did 'not accept or agree with' his deputy's view and that he intended to pursue a second referendum if Labour came into power, but would only choose a side once the shape of the Brexit deal became clear.

12 September 2019
Peter Brookes
The Times

14 September 2019
Steven Camley
Herald Scotland

Boris Johnson was forced to deny that he had lied to the Queen about his motivations for suspending Parliament in the run-up to the Brexit deadline. Johnson had claimed that proroguing Parliament was necessary to prepare for a new parliamentary session, but Scotland's highest civil court ruled that the suspension was 'unlawful' and motivated by the 'improper purpose of stymieing Parliament'. Johnson retorted, 'We need a Queen's Speech, we need to get on and do all sorts of things at a national level.'

With Parliament bitterly divided and Britain teetering on the edge of a no-deal departure from the EU, David Cameron broke his silence on Brexit in his autobiography, *For the Record*. In an interview prior to publication, Cameron accused former colleagues who backed the Leave campaign of 'trashing the government', turning it into a 'terrible Tory psychodrama' and claimed they had 'left the truth at home'. He also blamed himself for failing to see the bigger picture and for raising expectations too high for his renegotiation of EU membership.

15 September 2019
Scott Clissold
Sunday Express

Hendin's cartoon, which won the award for political cartoon of the year, was created after Boris Johnson's chaotic trip to Luxembourg to negotiate a Brexit agreement. Johnson was met with protestors shouting 'bollocks to Brexit' and 'bog off Boris' so loudly that he decided to forego a press conference with the country's prime minister, Xavier Bettel. Hendin remarks, 'The image of Bettel giving the conference beside an empty podium quickly became a viral image, so satirising it with an homage to K. C. Green's viral and famously memed "this is fine" comic seemed especially apt.'

17 September 2019
Rebecca Hendin
Guardian

The Liberal Democrat leader, Jo Swinson, asserted in her conference speech that her goal was to stop Brexit 'on day one' as prime minister. Swinson claimed that a parliamentary majority 'is for the taking . . . We can win. We must win. And to do so, we must build the biggest liberal movement this country has ever seen.' According to the cartoonist, 'It was party conference season, and Jo Swinson was saying that she was going to be prime minister and that the Lib Dems would be in government. I enjoy drawing her, though I do make her out to be a lot more evil than she actually is.'

18 September 2019
Peter Brookes
The Times

19 September 2019
Dave Brown
Independent

Labour's position on Brexit became even murkier after delegates at the annual party conference agreed to back Jeremy Corbyn's policy of remaining 'neutral' on how to resolve the Brexit question. Corbyn's policy was opposed by senior party members including John McDonnell, Keir Starmer and Emily Thornberry, and seemed to fly in the face of research showing that eight out of ten Labour supporters had voted to stay in the EU. Corbyn repeatedly refused to clarify his own personal opinion of Brexit, choosing to remain on the fence.

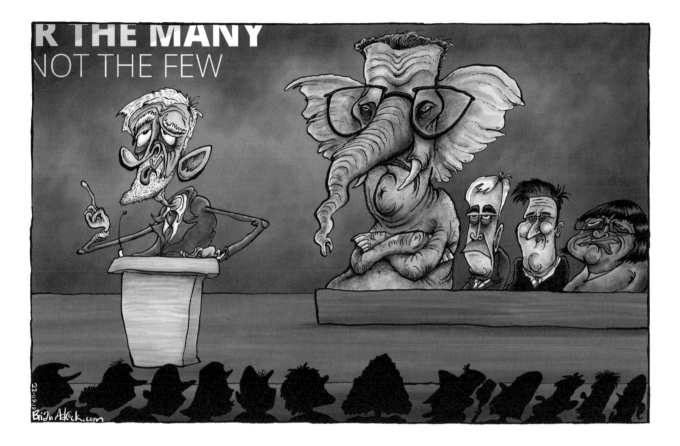

A 'drive-by shooting' designed to turn a 'broad church party' into one where 'pluralism isn't tolerated', was how Tom Watson described attempts to abolish his post of deputy leader at the Labour conference. The proposal had been tabled by Jon Lansman, of the pro-Corbyn group Momentum, at the party's ruling National Executive Committee. But the scheme was stymied by Corbyn himself who instead suggested that the post should merely be reviewed. In previous days, Watson had urged his party to 'unambiguously and unequivocally back Remain', in direct opposition to Corbyn's 'neutral' policy.

22 September 2019
Brian Adcock
Independent

According to the cartoonist, 'In stunning defiance of Boris Johnson's arrogant executive style, Lady Hale, as head of the Supreme Court, ruled that Johnson unlawfully advised the Queen to prorogue Parliament. The case went to the heart of principles of the British constitution, including the extent of a prime minister's power. All 11 Supreme Court judges unanimously found that they had the legal right to consider the reasons for prorogation, and that it was "unlawful, void and of no effect".' The president of the Supreme Court, Lady Hale, said that the judges could not find 'that there was any reason – let alone a good reason – to advise Her Majesty to prorogue Parliament for five weeks'.

27 September 2019
Andy Davey
Unpublished

After the Supreme Court ruling, Speaker John Bercow said that the House of Commons would reconvene immediately, allowing time the next day for 'urgent questions'. Jeremy Corbyn and Nicola Sturgeon both called on the prime minister to resign, but Boris Johnson merely commented that Brexit was 'not made much easier by this kind of stuff in Parliament or in the courts'.

25 September 2019
Patrick Blower
Daily Telegraph

MIND YOUR LANGUAGE...

BREXIT

26.9.19. DAVID SIMONDS

In a heated Commons debate, Boris Johnson had to be asked to moderate his language after he used the terms 'surrender', 'capitulation', 'traitor' and 'treason' to describe legislation to block a no-deal Brexit. Citing the murder of MP Jo Cox, as well as abuse repeatedly received by other members and their families, MP Paula Sherriff asked the prime minister to 'not resort to using offensive, dangerous or inflammatory language for legislation that we do not like'. Johnson responded, 'I have to say, Mr Speaker, that I have never heard so much humbug in my life.'

26 September 2019
Dave Simonds
Evening Standard

Boris Johnson termed himself 'the model of restraint' in reference to his language in the House of Commons. Around the same time he was referred to a police watchdog after a *Sunday Times* report claimed that Jennifer Arcuri was given preferential treatment and £10,000 in sponsorship cash from an organisation Johnson was responsible for as London mayor. The prime minister also denied groping a journalist's leg when he was editor of the *Spectator*.

30 September 2019
Morten Morland
The Times

3 October 2019
Christian Adams
Evening Standard

At the beginning of October, the prime minister published his plans for a Brexit deal, revealing that Northern Ireland could be tied to the EU single market whilst also leaving the customs union. In his letter to the president of the European Commission, Jean-Claude Juncker, Boris Johnson said that he hoped his plans provided 'the basis for rapid negotiations towards a solution'. Juncker replied that there remained several 'problematic points'.

Home Secretary Priti Patel delivered one of the most hard-line speeches at the Tory party conference in Manchester. She announced plans to increase the number of police officers carrying Tasers and to introduce a points-based immigration system. Bell compares the conference to George Cruikshank's depiction of the Peterloo Massacre of 1819, where cavalry charged a peaceful protest of working-class people calling for parliamentary reform.

3 October 2019
Steve Bell
Guardian

American businesswoman Jennifer Arcuri was in the spotlight amid allegations that she received public money and preferential treatment while Boris Johnson was London mayor. The former model and pole dancer denied that she had received favours but said that she and Johnson had 'a very close bond'. Revealing that she had listed Johnson as 'Alex the Great' in her phone, Arcuri said that he had visited her flat a handful of times and refused to deny that they had had an extra-marital affair. 'Because the press has made me this objectified ex-model pole dancer, I am really not going to answer that question,' she said.

8 October 2019
Morten Morland
The Times

In the week that Pizza Express announced that it was on the verge of financial collapse, Boris Johnson received another blow when German Chancellor Angela Merkel told him that a Brexit deal was 'overwhelmingly unlikely', according to Number 10 sources. In response, the president of the European Council, Donald Tusk warned Johnson against starting a 'stupid blame game'.

9 October 2019
Christian Adams
Evening Standard

"Come back!............ We've got dirt on the Bidens?..."

10 October 2019
Steven Camley
Herald Scotland

Against the advice of his state and defence departments, Donald Trump announced that he was withdrawing support for Kurdish allies in Syria, paving the way for Turkey to launch a long-planned offensive. The president justified his decision by saying that Kurdish fighters 'didn't help us in the Second World War, they didn't help us with Normandy'. Kurdish forces had, however, fought alongside US troops in the fight against ISIS for nearly five years, losing roughly 11,000 fighters. In other news, Trump was accused of urging the Ukrainian president to investigate his political rival, the Democrat Joe Biden – an accusation that reignited calls for impeachment.

According to the cartoonist, 'There were growing calls for an early general election and Jeremy Corbyn kept saying that, yes, he wanted one. But we knew damn well he didn't really.' In the end, Corbyn shocked supporters when he declared that he was 'champing at the bit' to fight another election, and that he would encourage his party to vote for a general election once the Brexit delay had been agreed. It was widely believed that Corbyn's senior advisers were against going to the polls, with John McDonnell reportedly calling it a 'trap', and many Labour MPs fearing a catastrophic defeat.

11 October 2019
Peter Brookes
The Times

18 October 2019
Steven Camley
Herald Scotland

Boris Johnson appeared to be nearing a Brexit deal, but only after making significant concessions to the EU: the two sides agreed, in principle, to create a customs border down the Irish Sea. The prime minister argued to MPs that Northern Ireland would still be within the UK's customs territory. A similar deal had already been rejected by Theresa May as one that no British prime minister could accept.

BREXTINCTION REBELLION...

'Here we have the Brexinction Rebellion and the DUP's Arlene Foster launching her own protest against the government, who are trying to drag her off the carriage,' says the cartoonist. The cartoon depicts DUP leader Arlene Foster protesting against the government after she said she would refuse to consent to Boris Johnson's Brexit plans if they required Northern Ireland to remain in an EU customs union. Around the same time, British Transport Police launched an investigation after London commuters appeared to attack Extinction Rebellion protestors, dragging them from the roof of a Tube train in Canning Town before kicking them repeatedly.

18 October 2019
Peter Brookes
The Times

20 October 2019
Brian Adcock
Independent

Despite Boris Johnson's claims that the UK would definitely leave the EU in October, he was forced to request another extension. The Letwin amendment, which enjoyed the support of opposition parties, was brought forward by Sir Oliver Letwin to delay a vote on Boris Johnson's departure deal. The proposition had the effect of bringing into play the Benn Act, legislation that would force the government to request an extension from the EU.

In Spain, the remains of dictator Francisco Franco were exhumed from his vast mausoleum, 44 years after his death. One of the key pledges of Spain's socialist government was to move the remains to a simple grave, arguing that Spain should not continue to glorify a fascist dictator. Franco was formerly buried in the Valley of the Fallen, a monument carved into a mountain, which houses more than 30,000 dead from the Spanish Civil War, including thousands who were buried alongside their opponents without their families' consent. It was partly built by political prisoners whom Franco's regime forced to work on the project.

25 October 2019
Steve Bell
Guardian

Boris Johnson's wished-for election became a reality when the House of Commons voted 438 votes to 20 to approve the first December election since 1923. The prime minister said it was necessary that the public was 'given a choice' on the future of the country. Johnson had been seeking a general election in order to break the parliamentary deadlock that had already caused Brexit to be delayed until 2020. He said that the country needed to 'come together to get Brexit done'.

27 October 2019
Morten Morland
The Times

According to the cartoonist, 'Jeremy Corbyn is more or less cornered into accepting a general election . . . It's pretty obvious that, barring an earthquake, he will lose such an election. He thinks his shattering charisma and campaigning technique will produce a turnaround in the polls like it did (almost) in 2017 . . . but his MPs don't.' Indeed, many Labour ministers expressed misgivings over an election and more than 100 did not take part or abstained from voting for an election in the House of Commons. While Corbyn insisted that he was ready to 'launch the most ambitious and radical campaign for real change our country has ever seen', his critics suggested that endorsing a poll was akin to a turkey voting for Christmas.

30 October 2019
Andy Davey
Daily Telegraph

Boris Johnson rejected an alliance with Nigel Farage's Brexit Party after Donald Trump said the prime minister and Farage would make an 'unstoppable team'. In previous days, Farage had threatened that the Conservatives would have to fight a Brexit Party candidate in every seat if the government didn't drop their Brexit deal or join a 'Leave alliance'. Farage likened the prime minister's Brexit deal to a car with a gleaming bonnet but with Theresa May's failed deal beneath. 'It is a bad old Brexit. It is not taking back control of laws or money or borders', he said.

3 November 2019
Morten Morland
The Times

Nigel Farage alleged that he had been offered a peerage and 'all sorts of baubles' in order to persuade the Brexit Party to not run against the Tories in the general election. Farage also revealed that he would not be standing as a candidate in the election, saying he would better serve his cause by travelling the country. His critics suggested that Farage was running scared after opinion polls showed the Brexit Party lagging behind in the voters' favour.

4 November 2019
Christian Adams
Evening Standard

NOTHING TO SEE HERE... MOVE ALONG!

Boris Johnson was accused of a cover-up after he delayed a report into Russian interference in UK politics. The Intelligence and Security Committee, who compiled the report, wanted to make recommendations to safeguard the December election but said they had received no reason why Johnson was refusing to approve the report. The report is said to include evidence concerning Russian attempts to influence the outcome of the 2016 EU referendum and 2017 general election. Emily Thornberry, shadow foreign secretary, also raised questions concerning Dominic Cummings' time working in Russia and his ties to the group, Conservative Friends of Russia.

6 November 2019
Dave Brown
Independent

Jacob Rees-Mogg apologised after he suggested that victims of the Grenfell Tower blaze did not use 'common sense' to flee the building, even though they were advised by firefighters to stay put. The Grenfell United group called Rees-Mogg's comments 'extremely painful and insulting to bereaved families'. 72 people lost their lives in the fire in June 2017. An inquiry later confirmed that many could have survived if the London fire brigade had dropped its stay put policy sooner.

6 November 2019
Steve Bell
Guardian

THREE WISE MEN...

8 November 2019
Peter Brookes
The Times

Two former Labour MPs, Ian Austin and John Woodcock, urged voters to support Boris Johnson in the upcoming election, claiming Jeremy Corbyn was 'completely unfit' to lead. 'Decent, traditional, patriotic Labour voters should be voting for Boris Johnson', Austin said. Austin also claimed that Tom Watson had resigned as deputy leader due to a lack of faith in Corbyn's leadership and concerns about antisemitism in the party. Their statement came on the same day that a Jewish newspaper published a report saying most Jewish people believe Corbyn to be an antisemite, a claim he denies.

A 'fervent and passionate unionist' was how Boris Johnson described himself on a visit to the Tayto factory in Tandragee, Northern Ireland. Johnson was visiting the country to defend his Brexit deal, which he said allowed 'unfettered access from Northern Ireland to GB', even though critics claim the plan creates a border down the Irish Sea. When asked why he chose the famous Tayto Castle for his Northern Ireland stop, Johnson simply replied he 'loved the crisps'.

8 November 2019
Nicola Jennings
Guardian

A little over a week after threatening to punish Boris Johnson's 'sellout' Brexit deal, Nigel Farage dropped his plan to challenge Conservative-held seats after facing pressure to not divide Leave supporters. Farage expressed frustration that the government was not more thankful for this concession, saying 'I would have expected, having put country before party, to perhaps have got something back from the Conservatives.' Instead, Boris Johnson replied that Farage's actions showed 'a recognition that there's only one way to get Brexit done, and that's to vote for the Conservatives'.

12 November 2019
Christian Adams
Evening Standard

The government was accused of showing an 'utterly outrageous' lack of concern after severe flooding devastated parts of northern England. Boris Johnson said that recovery grants would be provided to more than 1,200 evacuated households but Jeremy Corbyn criticised the government for not declaring a national emergency. Johnson was filmed mopping up at a Specsavers store, although many pointed out that his handiwork appeared to be making the situation worse. 'I think the image of Boris Johnson trying to rid a country of a biblical sized flood with a floor mop is a perfect metaphor for his handling of Brexit', one Twitter user commented.

14 November 2019
Dave Brown
Independent

15 November 2019
Ben Jennings
Guardian

On the campaign trail, Priti Patel pledged that the Conservative Party would reduce immigration by introducing a points-based system to allow highly skilled professionals into the country whilst shutting out low-skilled workers. Patel said, 'This can only happen if people vote for a Conservative majority government so we can leave the EU with a deal.' Patel claimed that research showed net migration would 'surge' to 840,000 a year if Jeremy Corbyn became prime minister – a claim Labour dismissed as 'fake news'.

Providing free superfast broadband for all homes and businesses in the UK was a key pledge of the Labour Party's election campaign. To achieve this, Labour said it would introduce a tax on multinational corporations as well as nationalise the parts of BT that own the country's internet infrastructure. Jeremy Corbyn said his vision would 'bring communities together in an inclusive and connected society'. Conservatives said the headline-grabbing policy was merely designed to detract from Labour's divisions and would 'cost hardworking taxpayers tens of billions'.

17 November 2019
Scott Clissold
Sunday Express

As speculation swirled about his relationship with convicted sex offender Jeffrey Epstein, Prince Andrew gave an interview to the BBC to address allegations that he had sex with a teenage girl, Virginia Roberts. Roberts' claim that he had been 'profusely sweating' during their encounter was false, according to the Duke of York, as he had a condition that made it 'impossible for me to sweat'. The prince was criticised widely for an interview that commentators said demonstrated a 'lack of humanity or perspective'.

18 November 2019
Steve Bright
Sun

TORTURING SQUIRRELS...

According to the cartoonist, 'A social media post and fake newspaper article claiming Jo Swinson killed squirrels went viral. It was all a load of nonsense, but fun nonetheless to have her as a squirrel crying as she reads how disastrously her campaign is going.' There was more bad news for the Liberal Democrats as a poll showed that voters liked Jo Swinson less the more they saw of her, even Remain supporters. The High Court also rejected an attempt by the Lib Dems to gain a spot in ITV's televised debate.

21 November 2019
Peter Brookes
The Times

24 November 2019
Chris Riddell
Observer

The Labour Party's election manifesto promised to 'transform' the UK and renationalise the water, energy, rail and mail industries, in a plan that BBC economists estimated would add £83 billion to government spending by 2024. The Liberal Democrat manifesto promised to cancel Brexit, provide free childcare and legalise cannabis. However, the Conservative manifesto launch was thrown off kilter by a 'fake news' scandal. Boris Johnson failed to answer questions about misleading the public after an official Tory Twitter account was renamed 'factcheckUK' during a live debate. The account then published a series of Conservative claims along with the word 'Fact'.

During the first live election debate host Julie Etchingham questioned Boris Johnson and Jeremy Corbyn about the 'extraordinary' levels of spending that both major parties were proposing. Referring to Theresa May's quote from the last election that there was 'no magic money tree', Etchingham asked, 'Have you found a magic money tree, Mr Johnson?', and 'Have you found more than one of them, Mr Corbyn?' Johnson drew laughter from the crowd when he joked that Corbyn must have found 'a money forest'.

25 November 2019
Patrick Blower
Daily Telegraph

Jeremy Corbyn declined to apologise to the Jewish community after the chief rabbi, Ephraim Mirvis, criticised how the Labour Party had dealt with antisemitism claims. 'A new poison, sanctioned from the very top, has taken root', Mirvis said. According to Brookes, 'antisemitism continued to rear its ugly head within the Labour Party. Corbyn had been given a very rough ride during his Andrew Neil interview the day before, with a large part of it focused on what he was doing to tackle the issue. Corbyn simply could not escape it and his lack of action came to play a large part in the election result.'

27 November 2019
Peter Brookes
The Times

The Conservative Party threatened to review Channel 4's public service broadcasting licence when it replaced Boris Johnson with a melting ice sculpture during a debate on climate change. After Johnson declined to take part in the debate the Conservatives offered Michael Gove instead but, when he arrived at the debate with the prime minister's father Stanley Johnson, both were turned away. Channel 4 presenter Krishnan Guru-Murthy said, 'As we made clear from the start, this debate was for leaders only.'

29 November 2019
Christian Adams
Evening Standard

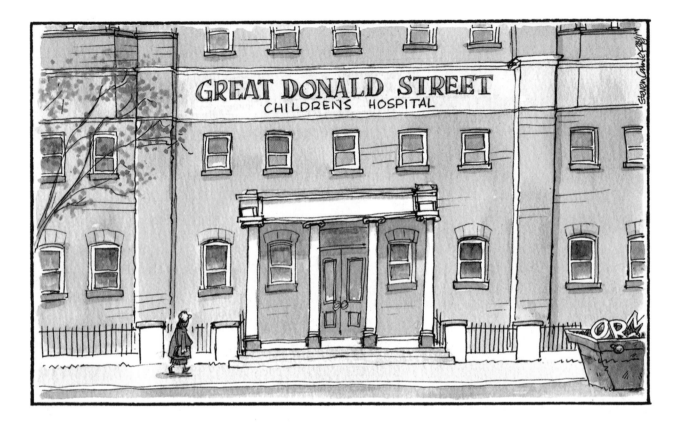

30 November 2019
Steven Camley
Herald Scotland

Jeremy Corbyn said that he had obtained official documents which showed that the NHS would be 'on the table' during post-Brexit trade talks with the US. The uncensored papers showed that 'under Boris Johnson the NHS is on the table and will be up for sale. He tried to cover it up in a secret agenda', according to Corbyn. The Conservative Party responded that the papers had been available online for several months and the claim that the NHS would be part of trade talks was 'nonsense'.

Boris Johnson refused to confirm whether he would take part in an interview with the BBC's Andrew Neil, who is widely regarded as one of the broadcaster's toughest interrogators. The Conservatives insisted they were 'in discussions' with the BBC over a possible interview but when Neil was asked if there had been any progress he replied 'None'. Labour accused Johnson of trying to avoid scrutiny – John McDonnell said the prime minister was sidestepping the interview because he knew Neil would 'take him apart'.

2 December 2019
Steve Bright
Sun

Boris Johnson was accused of 'trying to exploit' the London Bridge terror attack and turn it into an election issue. Two people were stabbed to death and several others were injured by Usman Khan, a convicted terrorist, before he was shot dead by police. The family of Jack Merritt, one of those murdered, called for the death of 'our beautiful, talented boy' not to be exploited for political gain. Even so, Johnson used the attack to call for hard-line reforms including mandatory minimum sentences for terrorists and an end to automatic early release. Johnson also claimed that a 'lefty government' had been responsible for Usman Khan's early release from prison.

2 December 2019
Ben Jennings
Guardian

The Labour Party said it would cut rail fares by 33 per cent if it won the election as part of a broader plan to renationalise the UK's rail network within five years. Labour estimated that it would save the average commuter £1,000 a year and represented the biggest ever reduction in rail fares. Transport Secretary Grant Shapps retorted that Corbyn's 'ideological plans would wreck our economy [and] cost people their livelihoods'. Labour's announcement was made on the same day that one of the longest train strikes in decades began. Members of the rail union RMT working for South Western Railway stopped working throughout December in a long-running dispute over the role of train guards.

3 December 2019
Patrick Blower
Daily Telegraph

President Trump has often been hostile to NATO – describing it as 'obsolete' and threatening to withdraw American support – but, in light of impeachment proceedings against him, he argued that his trip to a NATO summit was vitally important. Trump said that it was 'not nice' of Congress to schedule proceedings on the same week as his NATO trip and contended that all impeachment hearings should be postponed. 'Donald Trump had come out in defence of NATO during a press conference at the organisation's UK summit,' says Brookes. 'At the same time there were growing calls, soon to be realised, for Trump to be impeached. Here I have him calling in his NATO allies for a little extra support.'

5 December 2019
Peter Brookes
The Times

President Trump left a NATO summit early after a video emerged appearing to show other world leaders, including Boris Johnson, Justin Trudeau and Emmanuel Macron, joking at Trump's expense. In response, Trump said of Trudeau, 'He's two-faced . . . I find him to be a nice guy, but the truth is I called him out on the fact that he's not paying 2 per cent [of national GDP towards defence] and I guess he's not very happy about it.' One of the purposes of the summit was to discuss the threats posed by the rise of China and Russia and a joint statement by NATO leaders acknowledged the 'challenges' that Russia poses. However, earlier in the year, Trump had called Vladimir Putin a 'terrific person' and a 'great guy'.

6 December 2019
Kevin Kallaugher
Economist

PUDDING IS SERVED

7 December 2019
Dave Brown
Independent

Nancy Pelosi announced that the US House of Representatives would proceed with articles of impeachment against President Donald Trump. Trump was accused of withholding military aid to Ukraine in order to encourage the Ukrainian president to launch an investigation into Trump's political rival, Joe Biden. 'Our democracy is what is at stake', Pelosi said in a news conference. 'The president leaves us no choice but to act, because he is trying to corrupt, once again, the election.' The cartoon is inspired by a painting by Carlo Dolci, which shows Salome holding out the head of St. John the Baptist on a silver platter.

In homage to the Christmas classic *Love, Actually*, the Conservatives launched a campaign video with Boris Johnson starring in a recreation of the film's most iconic romantic scene. The 'Vote Conservative Actually' video showed Johnson silently presenting a woman with a series of Brexit-themed cards, including 'Your vote has never been more important, the other guy *could* win'. Jeremy Corbyn also released a pop-culture-themed video called 'Mean Tweets with Jeremy Corbyn', inspired by the US talk show host Jimmy Kimmel. Corbyn replied to one tweet in frustration, 'What is a commie hat? I wear a cap! It's a bit like when I was told I was riding a Maoist bicycle. It's a bicycle!'

11 December 2019
Patrick Blower
Daily Telegraph

In a disappointing election night for Labour, the party lost 8 per cent of their share of the national vote as well as 59 seats in Parliament. Jeremy Corbyn announced that he would stand down as party leader but not before a 'process of reflection'. The Conservative Party won a large majority by sweeping aside Labour strongholds in parts of northern England, the Midlands and Wales that had backed Brexit. Boris Johnson delivered a triumphant victory speech in front of a slogan reading 'The People's Government', saying Brexit was the 'irrefutable, irresistible, unarguable decision of the British people'. A day earlier Johnson had surprised JCB workers by driving a digger through a wall meant to represent the Brexit 'gridlock'.

13 December 2019
Christian Adams
Evening Standard

President Trump mocked teenage climate activist Greta Thunberg after she became *Time* magazine's youngest-ever Person of the Year. 'So ridiculous,' Trump tweeted. 'Greta must work on her anger management problem, then go to a good old fashioned movie with a friend! Chill Greta, Chill!' The Trump administration also posted an edited version of the *Time* cover, superimposing Trump's head onto Thunberg's body, and saying 'When it comes to keeping his promises, there's only one Person of the Year'. President Trump had been on the shortlist for this year's award. Thunberg merely responded by changing her Twitter bio to 'A teenager working on her anger management problem'.

13 December 2019
Steve Bell
Guardian

15 December 2019
Ben Jennings
Guardian

Boris Johnson's election victory was attributed to converting long-held Labour seats with a hard-line Brexit stance, including the former mining constituency of Blyth Valley which had been held by Labour since its creation. 'We have won from Workington to Woking,' Johnson said on election night, 'including seats the Conservatives have not won for 100 years or more. Wrexham. Tony Blair's old seat in Sedgefield. We turned Redcar Blue-car.' Johnson later paid a visit to Sedgefield to thank people for 'breaking the voting habits of generations', with voters chanting 'Boris, Boris, Boris' as the prime minister arrived.

Jeremy Corbyn and John McDonnell both apologised for the Labour Party's election defeat but also blamed the media. Corbyn said he was 'sorry that we came up short', but defended his 'historically important' campaign against the media's 'personal abuse'. Talking to the BBC, McDonnell said he 'owns this disaster' but also blamed the media portrayal of the party, saying 'anyone who stands up for real change will be met by the full force of media opposition.' However, many within the party blamed the leadership. Former Home Secretary Alan Johnson protested that Corbyn 'couldn't lead the working class out of a paper bag'.

17 December 2019
Patrick Blower
Daily Telegraph

As the Labour leadership contest began in earnest, Sir Keir Starmer rejected claims that he was too middle-class for the role. 'My dad worked in a factory, he was a toolmaker and my mum was a nurse,' Starmer said. 'Actually, my background isn't what people think it is. I had actually never been in any other workplace other than a factory until I left university.' The leadership contest was compared by some to the Monty Python sketch *The Four Yorkshiremen*, in which the characters try to outdo each other's stories of humble beginnings.

19 December 2019
Peter Brookes
The Times

Jeremy Corbyn's 'process of reflection' quickly turned into a factional leadership race, with many of the potential contenders keen to distance themselves from his tenure. Emily Thornberry said that Corbyn had been 'really badly let down by people who advised him', Yvette Copper said 'we clearly have to change', while Sir Keir Starmer said Labour didn't '[tackle] the "get Brexit done" slogan strongly enough'. Corbyn also faced calls to leave his leadership post early – MP Margaret Hodge tweeted, 'Corbyn talking about a period of "reflection". I've reflected. You failed. Please stand down.'

20 December 2019
Dave Simonds
Evening Standard

Despite losing his Richmond Park seat in the general election, Zac Goldsmith was given a life peerage so that he could keep his role as environment minister. Goldsmith, son of the billionaire businessman James Goldsmith, has long been an ally and friend of Prime Minister Boris Johnson and his partner Carrie Symonds. The shadow Cabinet Office minister, Jon Trickett, said, 'It says everything you need to know about Boris Johnson's respect for democracy that he has ignored the voters of Richmond Park and appointed Goldsmith to government.'

21 December 2019
Peter Brookes
The Times

According to the cartoonist, 'Boris Johnson planned a big shift of civil servants out of London, notably by placing new government agencies outside the UK capital, as part of his efforts to "level up" opportunity and spread wealth across the country . . . [Johnson] pledged to close the "opportunity gap" between rich and poor, notably by boosting the regions, and he is now under pressure to deliver after the Conservatives won seats traditionally held by Labour, notably in the Midlands and northern England. You could see it as a cynical, vote-retaining boost to these newly-won northern seats.'

28 December 2019
Andy Davey
Daily Telegraph

Boris Johnson used his Christmas message to urge the UK to 'celebrate the good that is to come' by 'tucking into some delicious food'. Johnson and his partner, Carrie Symonds, later jetted off to the island of Mustique to celebrate New Year. Jennings here shows Johnson gorging on 'Democracy' while, as the cartoonist notes, 'Dominic Cummings looks on'. The cartoon is based on James Gillray's 'A voluptuary under the horrors of digestion' which mocked the Prince of Wales, later to rule as George IV, for his lavish lifestyle.

29 December 2019
Nicola Jennings
Guardian

The government was forced to apologise after it accidently published the addresses of over 1,000 of the New Year Honours recipients online. Sir Elton John, cricketer Ben Stokes, former Conservative Party leader Iain Duncan Smith, TV chef Nadiya Hussain and senior police officers investigating the Salisbury poisonings were all among those affected. According to the cartoonist, 'This was drawn on a Sunday between Christmas and New Year. Not usually a time of year when it's easy to find an interesting subject. The story was a bit of a storm in a teacup, but it was a bit of fun, and it had a seasonal flavour.'

30 December 2019
Peter Schrank
The Times

HOPE

'I wanted to produce a hopeful image for the start of the new year. But with forest fires raging in Australia, no action on climate change and the ongoing refugee crisis, it was difficult to find any optimism,' says the cartoonist. 'I was struck by how much hope was being invested in Greta Thunberg and what a huge amount of weight she was bearing for the climate movement on her shoulders.' The cartoon – showing Thunberg facing off political leaders and the bosses of the world's most polluting companies – suggests 'what a slim figure of hope Thunberg represents, in such desperate circumstances'.

2 January 2020
Henny Beaumont
Guardian

The Iranian general Qasem Soleimani was killed in a Baghdad airstrike ordered by Donald Trump. Analysts said that the attack risked destabilising the region, because the general was widely considered the second most powerful person in Iran. As the president's critics accused him of undermining the US's strategy in the Middle East, Trump responded to the news by tweeting an image of the American flag.

5 January 2020
Chris Riddell
Observer

6 January 2020
Ben Jennings
Guardian

Boris Johnson urged Donald Trump to 'de-escalate' mounting tensions with Iran, as relations soured following the assassination of Qasem Soleimani. Returning from a new year's break in the Caribbean, the prime minister said that Soleimani was 'responsible for a pattern of disruptive, destabilising behaviour' as head of Iran's international military operations. But he urged the US president to take steps to prevent war, saying, 'It is clear that all calls for retaliation or reprisals will simply lead to more violence.'

THE ROAD TO VICTORY

Blower 8·1·20

Rebecca Long Bailey announced her intention to succeed Jeremy Corbyn as leader of the Labour Party. She was the sixth candidate to throw her hat in the ring after Keir Starmer, Emily Thornberry, Lisa Nandy, Jess Phillips and Clive Lewis. The three-month leadership election looked set to revolve around how to recover from the devastating defeat in December's general election.

8 January 2020
Patrick Blower
Daily Telegraph

10 January 2020
Kevin Kallaugher
Economist

Australian premier Scott Morrison was criticised over his climate policy, as bushfires spread across the country. Following the hottest and driest year since records began, an unprecedented number of fires broke out on the eastern and southern coasts, burning over 6 million hectares by mid-January. Critics said the bushfires demonstrated how Morrison had failed on global warming, by continuing to invest in fossil fuels and downplaying the risks of climate change.

The Duke and Duchess of Sussex announced their intention to step back as 'senior royals'. In a post on their Instagram page, Harry and Meghan indicated they wanted to reduce their official duties to the Crown and 'work to become financially independent'. Commentators noted the couple's recent use of the brand 'Sussex Royal', suggesting the pair could make their money from lucrative sponsorship deals with private companies.

11 January 2020
Peter Brookes
The Times

15 January 2020
Dave Brown
Independent

Pro-Brexit MPs backed calls for Big Ben to chime at 11pm on 31 January, to mark the moment Britain would formally leave the EU. The Palace of Westminster's iconic bell had been largely silent since 2017, when a major renovation project began. But Boris Johnson floated the idea of crowdfunding the £500,000 it would cost to chime the bell on 'Brexit Day' as a one-off, and the Tory MP Mark Francois pledged £1,000 to the cause.

Health Secretary Matt Hancock indicated the government was considering scrapping the four-hour waiting time target in A&E. NHS guidance said that all hospitals should aim to treat emergency patients within four hours of them arriving, but many had been falling short due to mounting pressures on the health service. After Hancock suggested that an alternative, 'clinically appropriate' objective may be preferable, Labour accused the government of 'moving the goalposts' on the issue.

16 January 2020
Steve Bell
Guardian

17 January 2020
Peter Brookes
The Times

Vladimir Putin appeared in the Russian State Duma to back an amendment that would allow him to run again for president in 2024. The Russian premier, who has been president or prime minister for two decades, spoke in favour of amending a constitutional ban that prevented him standing for a third consecutive mandate.

Labour leadership contender Rebecca Long Bailey won the endorsement of the Unite trade union, cementing her position as the candidate preferred by the left of the party. Unite's general secretary, Len McCluskey, said the shadow education secretary had 'both the brains and the brilliance to take on Boris Johnson'. But Long Bailey's critics within Labour said she was the preferred candidate of Johnson, thanks to her close links with the defeated incumbent Jeremy Corbyn.

19 January 2020
Scott Clissold
Sunday Express

THE EXPULSION...

20 January 2020
Morten Morland
The Times

The Duke and Duchess of Sussex gave up their royal titles following their decision to step down as 'senior royals'. Harry and Meghan agreed to stop using the prefixes His and Her Royal Highness and to stop participating in most Crown functions. At a charity dinner Prince Harry indicated that he had hoped to continue in some duties, but had been told this 'wasn't possible'. The comments fuelled further speculation about a rift between the Sussexes and the Queen, as indicated in this reworking of Masaccio's masterpiece *The Expulsion from the Garden of Eden* (c. 1425).

Government sources indicated that Boris Johnson wanted to move the House of Lords permanently to York. According to the *Sunday Times*, the prime minister had asked civil servants to investigate the practicalities of relocating the Lords, a move he thought would help cement the Conservative Party's recent success in the North. Critics said the move didn't go far enough in reorganising the unelected upper house, which advocates of constitutional reform view as anachronistic.

20 January 2020
Brian Adcock
Independent

22 January 2020
Steven Camley
Herald Scotland

Donald Trump used his speech at the World Economic Forum to denounce 'prophets of doom' on climate change, a comment widely interpreted as a dig at audience member Greta Thunberg. The teenage climate activist had earlier told the meeting of political and business leaders in Davos, Switzerland, that their inaction on the climate crisis was 'fuelling the flames by the hour'.

Monty Python's Terry Jones died at the age of 77. One of Jones' best-known roles was Brian's mother in *Life of Brian* (1979). In his most famous sketch Jones shouts from his window to a crowd of worshippers, 'He's not the Messiah, he's a very naughty boy.'

23 January 2020
Steven Camley
Herald Scotland

29 January 2020
Peter Brookes
The Times

Boris Johnson approved plans to allow the Chinese tech giant Huawei to play a limited role in building the UK's 5G internet network. The decision was controversial due to security concerns about the company's links with the Chinese government. Meanwhile, the Foreign Office urged Britons not to go to China, as the country struggled to contain a highly contagious new disease called coronavirus.

TAKE AWAY...

FCK PALESTINIANS

BIG BARGAIN BUCKET

Donald Trump outlined a new plan for peace in the Middle East, offering a raft of concessions to the Israeli government regarding its relationship with Palestine. The US president backed plans to establish Jerusalem as Israel's 'undivided' capital city, and to acknowledge most Israeli settlements on occupied Palestinian land. Although the plan did offer a route to statehood for Palestine, most Palestinian leaders criticised the plan as an assault on their sovereignty. However, the Israeli president Benjamin Netanyahu welcomed the announcement as 'a great plan for Israel, a great plan for peace'.

30 January 2020
Dave Brown
Independent

2 February 2020
Chris Riddell
Observer

Britain formally left the European Union on 31 January. According to the *Mail on Sunday*, Boris Johnson celebrated the UK's departure by drinking a £350 bottle of wine, while his chief adviser Dominic Cummings wept with joy. Anti-Brexit MPs said that Johnson's confidence was misplaced, considering the scale of the task ahead – not least the need to work out a new trade deal with the EU.

The Democratic Party's presidential caucus in Iowa ended in turmoil due to problems with its vote-counting technology. The ballot of party members in the mid-western state was supposed to offer a sense of who the Democrats might choose as their presidential candidate, from a packed field that included Bernie Sanders, Pete Buttigieg and Elizabeth Warren. But faults with the software used to collect members' votes caused an embarrassing delay in the announcement of the results.

4 February 2020
Christian Adams
Evening Standard

One of Boris Johnson's aides banned unsympathetic reporters from attending a Downing Street briefing. The prime minister's most senior communications adviser sparked an outcry for trying to exclude reporters from the *Mirror, i, Huffington Post, PoliticsHome* and *Independent* from an official press conference. Critics said the prime minister was trying to stop pro-Remain and liberal voices from reporting on his policies – as hinted by Dave Brown's reworking of this famous post-war photo from a bed and breakfast window.

5 February 2020
Dave Brown
Independent

Senior Democrat Nancy Pelosi, the Speaker of the House of Representatives, tore up Donald Trump's State of the Union speech moments after he had finished delivering it. As Congress applauded the president for his 75-minute speech, Pelosi picked up a copy and ripped it in two. Commentators suggested the move would do little to harm Trump, whose impeachment was abandoned a day later when he was acquitted by the Republican-controlled Senate.

6 February 2020
Peter Brookes
The Times

Boris Johnson's father, Stanley Johnson, accidentally revealed that he had been speaking to the Chinese ambassador about the coronavirus outbreak. The news broke after Stanley Johnson inadvertently copied a BBC employee into an email intended for UK government officials, in which he expressed concern that his son had not yet spoken to the Chinese about the disease. A government spokesperson said the UK had been in frequent contact with Beijing since the outbreak began.

Boris Johnson instructed civil servants to investigate building a bridge between Scotland and Northern Ireland. Critics said that it was impossible to construct the bridge, with one engineer branding the scheme 'as feasible as building a bridge to the moon'. Meanwhile, the opposition continued to attack Johnson for handing too much power to his chief adviser, Dominic Cummings.

11 February 2020
Brian Adcock
Independent

12 February 2020
Steve Bell
Guardian

Downing Street defended a deportation flight to Jamaica, saying that concerns over its legality were a 'Westminster bubble' issue. A court judgment had ordered the government to remove over half of the people on the flight list, ruling that their deportation was unlawful. But the chancellor, Sajid Javid, said that fears about the flight were unfounded, describing its passengers as 'all foreign national offenders'.

Boris Johnson confirmed that the HS2 high-speed rail link between London and the North would be built as planned. The government had placed the scheme under review due to extensive criticism over its cost and management. Commentators pointed out that Johnson – who famously once said he would lie down in front of bulldozers to prevent a third runway at Heathrow – had a penchant for major infrastructure projects. He had previously backed an airport in the Thames Estuary ('Boris Island'), a cable car from Greenwich to Docklands in London, and a Scotland–Northern Ireland bridge.

12 February 2020
Dave Brown
Independent

According to the cartoonist, 'Bernie Sanders won the New Hampshire Democratic primary contest on a terrible night for Joe Biden. He prevailed over centrist former mayor Pete Buttigieg. Elizabeth Warren and Joe Biden, the two frontrunners, finished in fourth and fifth places. Sanders declared the night "the beginning of the end" of Trump, even though there was a long way to go – and, as it turned out, Sanders' presidential hopes were short-lived.'

13 February 2020
Andy Davey
Daily Telegraph

Boris Johnson created a newly unified team of advisers to the Treasury and Number 10, in a decision widely credited to his chief adviser Dominic Cummings. The chancellor, Sajid Javid, resigned over the plan. In his resignation statement, Javid said that the prime minister needed to have teams with the 'integrity that you would wish to be associated with' – a comment interpreted as a dig at Cummings.

14 February 2020
Steven Camley
Herald Scotland

15 February 2020
Chris Duggan
The Times

'The nation's favourite éminence grise, working behind the scenes in restructuring government, clashed with the hapless new chancellor, Sajid Javid, who was forced to resign rather than sack his own team of advisers,' says the cartoonist. 'In his resignation speech he decided not to talk about who was behind these "comings and goings", as he described them.'

Government sources hinted that Downing Street was planning on scrapping the BBC licence fee and forcing the state broadcaster to adopt a subscription model. The policy would represent the biggest shake-up at the BBC in decades, and was attributed to Number 10 adviser Dominic Cummings – who, in a blog post from before he worked for the government, had called for the 'end of the BBC in its current form'.

16 February 2020
Ben Jennings
Guardian

Social care providers expressed concern about the government's proposed new immigration system, saying it would lead to a labour shortage in care homes. Under the new rules, few care workers would qualify to enter the country – even though a large proportion of current carers are immigrants. Boris Johnson's critics said he had given up on trying to solve the social care crisis, despite having said he wanted to end it 'once and for all' in his first speech as prime minister.

20 February 2020
Peter Brookes
The Times

Boxer Tyson Fury defeated Deontay Wilder to become the heavyweight world boxing champion. And he wasn't the only apparently unstoppable force: left-winger Bernie Sanders cemented his position as front-runner to be the 2020 Democratic presidential candidate at the Nevada primary, while the Italian government struggled to stop the spread of coronavirus through the population.

24 February 2020
Brian Adcock
Independent

25 February 2020
Ian Knox
Belfast Telegraph

A hearing began in London for the extradition of Julian Assange, the founder of WikiLeaks. Assange is wanted in the US on charges of attempted hacking and breaches of the Espionage Act, related to the publication of hundreds of thousands of diplomatic files, including those covering US activities in Afghanistan and Iraq. Assange's legal team argue that his life would be endangered if extradited as he is viewed as 'an enemy of America who must be brought down'. They also suggested the extradition request was politically motivated. The US government says that, by publishing unredacted documents, Assange willingly put human rights activists, dissidents and journalists living abroad at serious risk of harm.

Harvey Weinstein was convicted of rape at his trial in New York City. The former Holly-wood producer had been accused of sexual misconduct by over 80 women, becoming the most high-profile culprit in the global #MeToo movement. Donald Trump welcomed the verdict for sending a 'very strong message' – though critics said the president had not adequately rebutted his own allegations of sexual harassment.

26 February 2020
Steve Bell
Guardian

BROTHERS IN ARMS

29 February 2020
Ingram Pinn
Financial Times

Donald Trump went on his first state visit to India, feting Prime Minister Narendra Modi as an 'exceptional leader' and 'my true friend'. The US president's trip proved controversial, coming in the wake of growing tensions across India brought about by Modi's policy towards Muslims. Towards the end of Trump's visits, the worst riots in decades broke out in Delhi in response to the ruling BJP's controversial new citizenship bill, widely known as the 'anti-Muslim law'.

Donald Trump appointed his vice president, Mike Pence, to oversee the US's response to the coronavirus pandemic, telling the public that the risk from the disease 'remains very low'. According to the cartoonist, 'I don't really enjoy drawing Trump. His awfulness is beyond the reach of my pen. Although putting him in his bedroom, in front of Fox News and bingeing on junk food can help. Giving him his square and dense vice president for company helps too.'

2 March 2020
Peter Schrank
The Times

TO SHAKE OR NOT TO SHAKE...

Blower 3.3.20

3 March 2020
Patrick Blower
Daily Telegraph

Boris Johnson told journalists that he 'shook hands with everybody' during a recent hospital visit, despite growing evidence that reducing physical contact would slow the spread of coronavirus. Meanwhile, the UK began trade deal talks with the EU, with Europe's lead negotiator Michel Barnier reminding the British government that they had agreed to align with EU rules on subsidies and standards.

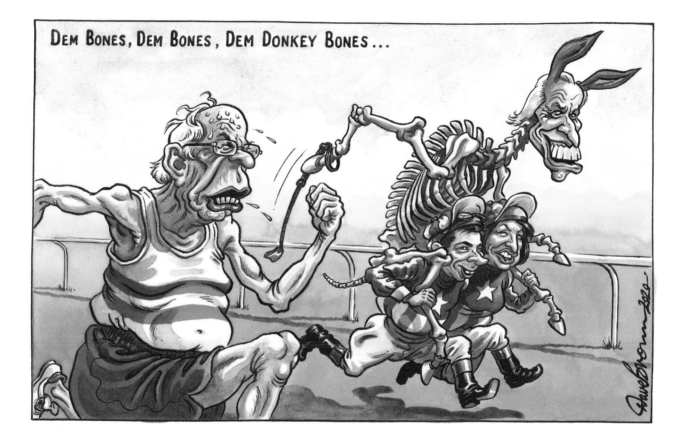

DEM BONES, DEM BONES, DEM DONKEY BONES...

Joe Biden regained his position as frontrunner for the Democratic presidential nomination, winning in 10 of 14 states to declare on 'Super Tuesday'. In the lead-up to the vote, commentators had suggested that Biden's campaign was flagging, with the left-winger Bernie Sanders looking increasingly likely to win. But Biden was buoyed by the endorsements of centrists Pete Buttigieg and Amy Klobuchar, who both pulled out of the race less than 24 hours before the vote.

5 March 2020
Dave Brown
Independent

5 March 2020
Steve Bell
Guardian

Boris Johnson defended the home secretary, Priti Patel, after fresh bullying allegations emerged. With Patel sitting beside him at Prime Minister's Questions, the prime minister said that Patel was doing an 'outstanding' job. Steve Bell's cartoon treatment of the incident proved controversial, with some suggesting it was insensitive to depict Patel with a bull's nose ring, considering her Hindu background. The former chancellor, Sajid Javid, took to Twitter to describe the cartoon as 'incredibly offensive'.

As several European states went into lockdown in response to coronavirus, Boris Johnson rejected claims that his approach to the disease was too hands-off. The prime minister said the government was trying to 'put out' new cases of the disease, but emphasised that the single most important change required was for people to frequently wash their hands 'for the length of time it takes to sing Happy Birthday twice'. Critics said the government was too preoccupied with Brexit and the impending budget to respond adequately to the developing pandemic.

8 March 2020
Chris Riddell
Observer

HIGH SEASON...

after CANALETTO

10 March 2020
Christian Adams
Evening Standard

Photos of an eerily deserted Venice circulated online, after the city's usually tourist-filled streets and canals were emptied by the coronavirus lockdown. Italy had become the first European country to experience the full brunt of the disease, with the whole country entering lockdown on 9 March and with the north of the country particularly hard hit. The surreal images inspired Christian Adams to reimagine Canaletto's *The Bucintoro at the Molo on Ascension Day* (*c.* 1733–4) devoid of people.

The Premier League suspended all events to try to slow the spread of coronavirus. The decision came a day after Boris Johnson said the government was considering banning all sporting fixtures. The BBC reported that Football Association bosses feared they would need to abandon the UK football season altogether.

14 March 2020
Ben Jennings
Guardian

PSSST....!

LUXURY ORGANIC

3 PLY SCENTED

PADDED VEGAN

17 March 2020
Brian Adcock
Independent

Panic buying spread across the UK, amidst rumours that the UK's food supply would be adversely affected by the impending coronavirus lockdown. Supermarkets placed limits on high-demand items including pasta, soap, long-life milk and, above all, toilet paper after footage circulated online of shelves emptied of key supplies.

As airlines around the world cancelled flights in response to the escalating coronavirus crisis, the chief executive of British Airways said the pandemic was a problem of 'global proportions like no other we have known'. Bosses at airlines including BA, RyanAir and EasyJet grounded planned flights in response to collapsing demand and increasingly strict travel restrictions.

17 March 2020
Steve Bright
Sun

18 March 2020
Patrick Blower
Daily Telegraph

On 16 March, Boris Johnson urged Britons to avoid going to all social venues, and called on them to work from home wherever possible. The government would go on to formally close all cafés, bars and restaurants on 20 March, and announce a strictly enforced lockdown on 23 March. The new policy led to eerily empty bars across the nation – reminiscent, in Patrick Blower's view, of Edward Hopper's evocative painting *Nighthawks* (1942).

Boris Johnson issued strict new guidance preventing Britons leaving the house in all but 'very limited' circumstances. Under the new anti-coronavirus measures, it was prohibited to go out except for one form of exercise per day, medical requirements, and to commute where 'absolutely necessary'. Having been announced on 23 March, the restrictions became legally enforceable on 26 March.

24 March 2020
Brian Adcock
Independent

Chancellor Rishi Sunak unveiled a raft of new policies designed to keep the UK economy afloat during the coronavirus crisis. Describing the package as 'unprecedented in the history of the British state', on 20 March Sunak outlined a furlough scheme that would pay 80 per cent of the wages of staff put on leave. A week later, he extended a version of the scheme to self-employed workers. Commentators pointed out the parallels between the Conservatives' radical interventions and those proposed by Jeremy Corbyn's Labour Party at the general election.

27 March 2020
Peter Brookes
The Times

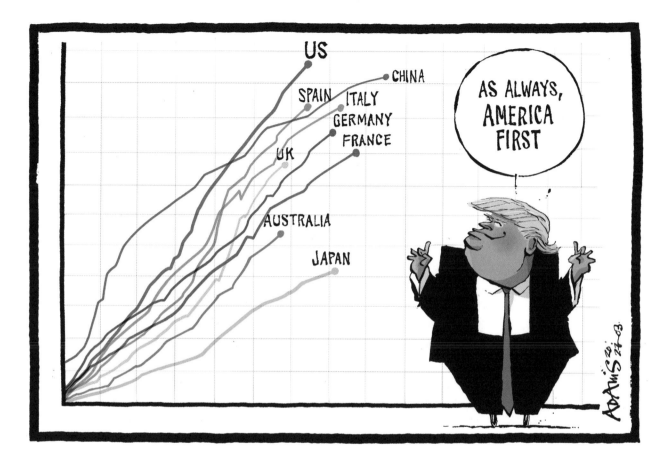

The United States surpassed China and Italy to become the country with the most cases of coronavirus. Since the arrival of the disease in America, Donald Trump had adopted a hands-off approach, leaving policy to individual states and frequently calling for Americans to return to work. Trump attributed the high number of positive cases to 'the amount of testing that we're doing', and reiterated his prediction that the country would return to work 'pretty quickly'.

27 March 2020
Christian Adams
Evening Standard

27 March 2020
Dave Brown
Independent

The government faced criticism for failing to find sufficient personal protective equipment (PPE) for use in UK hospitals. As reports came in of doctors and nurses being forced to go without masks and gloves, it emerged that the British government had passed up an opportunity to participate in an EU scheme to procure PPE. Critics accused Boris Johnson of failing to take up the EU offer for ideological reasons.

"A BEAUTIFUL TIMELINE"

Donald Trump outlined his strategy for the US to ease its lockdown restrictions in time for Easter Sunday on April 12, hailing the plan as 'a beautiful timeline'. The president reiterated his opposition to staying in lockdown for too long, saying that 'you can destroy a country this way, by closing it down'. But critics said his plan was naïve at a time when the US had the highest number of coronavirus cases of any country on Earth.

28 March 2020
Ingram Pinn
Financial Times

Over three quarters of a million people volunteered to help the NHS in its fight against coronavirus. On 24 March, the health secretary called for 250,000 people to support the health service through the pandemic – calling on everyone from retired doctors to untrained members of the public to answer the call for help. By the end of the week, more than three times that number had signed up. Clissold references David Low's famous cartoon from May 1940, *All Behind You, Winston*, which depicts members of the coalition government marching behind Winston Churchill after he became prime minister in the first year of the Second World War.

29 March 2020
Scott Clissold
Sunday Express

Boris Johnson and the health secretary, Matt Hancock, tested positive for coronavirus. Meanwhile, the Scottish secretary, Alister Jack, and the chief medical officer, Chris Whitty, went into self-isolation with coronavirus symptoms. Standing in for the prime minister at the government's daily press conference, Michael Gove said the developments showed that the virus 'does not discriminate', but emphasised that the prime minister remained well enough to lead the UK's coronavirus response remotely.

31 March 2020
Morten Morland
The Times

The government wrote to 30 million households across the UK urging Britons to stay at home to protect the NHS. The letter, signed by Boris Johnson, reiterated the message of his earlier televised addresses, giving 'one simple instruction – you must stay at home'. Days after sending the letter, the prime minister was moved to intensive care after his coronavirus symptoms worsened.

1 April 2020
Dave Brown
Independent

President Jair Bolsonaro called on Brazilians to continue to go about their daily business even as cases of coronavirus continued to climb. He downplayed the risks of the illness, calling it a 'little flu', and criticised state governors who had imposed regional lockdowns. There had been 1,000 confirmed deaths from coronavirus in the country by the beginning of April.

3 April 2020
Kevin Kallaugher
Economist

SHOES TO FILL...

Keir Starmer won the election to become leader of the Labour Party. The former shadow Brexit secretary beat rivals Rebecca Long Bailey and Lisa Nandy, gaining 56 per cent of the vote in the first round. In a pre-recorded video message, Starmer said his goal was to lead Labour 'into a new era with confidence and hope'. Critics said that, considering Labour's catastrophic 2019 election result, he would struggle to do worse than his predecessor Jeremy Corbyn.

4 April 2020
Morten Morland
The Times

Caught With Our Trousers Down

According to the cartoonist, 'Other countries responded quickly to the pandemic (good examples being South Korea and Germany), and their actions were reflected in low fatality figures. Whereas by the time the magnitude of the situation became apparent in the UK, Brits had moved into panic-buying mode – emptying supermarket shelves, especially of toilet rolls, as the country figuratively, and presumably literally, shat itself. Given the disastrous results of our flat-footedness, perhaps we had every reason to.'

4 April 2020
Chris Duggan
The Times

5 April 2020
Ben Jennings
Guardian

Weather forecasters predicted a week of warm sunshine over the Easter weekend – though many Britons would have to remain inside throughout. Reports indicated that the lockdown regulations were being followed closely, with most of the public staying in for all but essential trips.

Scotland's chief medical officer, Dr Catherine Calderwood, resigned for not adhering to coronavirus guidelines. Calderwood said she was 'truly sorry' for visiting her second home in Fife during the lockdown. First Minister Nicola Sturgeon at first backed Calderwood to keep her job, but she ultimately stood down due to the 'justifiable focus on my behaviour risks becoming a distraction'.

6 April 2020
Steven Camley
Herald Scotland

The former Labour leader Ed Miliband was appointed shadow business and energy secretary by Keir Starmer. Miliband said he was pleased to return to the frontbench, remarking that the coronavirus recovery was an opportunity to 'reshape our economy, addressing the insecurity many millions of workers face'. Critics said that Miliband – who was famously snapped messily eating a bacon sandwich during the 2015 general election – might undermine Starmer's attempts to 'detoxify' the party.

8 April 2020
Peter Brookes
The Times

Donald Trump pulled US funding for the World Health Organization, saying the corona-virus pandemic showed it had 'failed in its basic duty'. The president said the WHO had helped cover up the spread of the virus due to its supposed political proximity to China. Trump also came under fire for hailing an anti-malaria drug as a 'gamechanger' in tackling the illness. He encouraged Americans to take hydroxychloroquine, despite no conclusive evidence it was an effective treatment.

9 April 2020
Dave Brown
Independent

13 April 2020
Brian Adcock
Independent

Boris Johnson left hospital after a week, having spent three days in intensive care being treated for coronavirus. A spokesperson said Johnson would not immediately return to work, and instead would convalesce in his country residence, Chequers. Meanwhile, the government came under fire for its rollout of personal protective equipment to medical professionals, amidst ongoing reports of shortages in hospitals across the UK.

Matt Hancock was criticised by NHS professionals for implying that they were using too much personal protective equipment. The health secretary implored people to only 'use the equipment they clinically need . . . no more and no less' – a comment many took as a dig at health workers. 'On this occasion I tried to come up with something clever, but none of my ideas impressed the editor,' says the cartoonist. 'Based on a suggestion from him I came up with this. It seemed a bit obvious to me, but that's not necessarily a bad thing. Better to be obvious and comprehensible than clever and obscure.'

14 April 2020
Peter Schrank
The Times

21 April 2020
Morten Morland
The Times

Harry and Meghan said they would stop cooperating with the UK tabloid press. The Duke and Duchess of Sussex sent a letter to the editors of the *Sun*, *Mail*, *Express* and *Mirror*, saying they refused to participate in 'an economy of clickbait and distortion'. The comments were criticised by some journalists, with David Yelland, former editor of the *Sun*, attacking the couple for making the story 'all about me' in the midst of a pandemic.

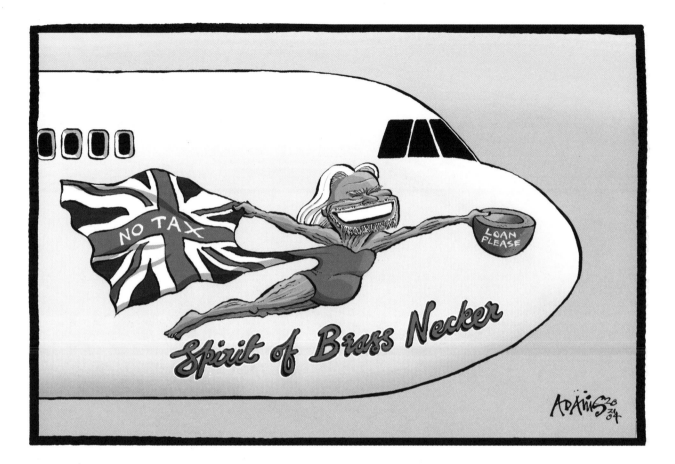

Richard Branson requested an emergency government loan of £500 million for his airline Virgin Atlantic, which had been hard hit by the coronavirus travel ban. Branson's critics said he had no right to a government loan, pointing out that he had paid no UK income tax for 14 years. Branson has long denied being a tax exile, and said that he left the country not for tax reasons but due to 'love of the beautiful British Virgin Islands and in particular [his home] Necker Island'.

21 April 2020
Christian Adams
Evening Standard

23 April 2020
Peter Brookes
The Times

MPs participated in the first ever virtual Prime Minister's Questions. Under new rules drafted by the Leader of the House of Commons, Jacob Rees-Mogg, no more than 120 MPs were allowed in the house at one time, and they were all encouraged to stay two metres apart. MPs who could not attend were able to ask questions via video-link.

Donald Trump was ridiculed for suggesting that coronavirus patients could be treated by injecting disinfectant into their bodies. 'What a guy! Tremendous person! Bigly!' says the cartoonist. 'Anyway, the world is asked to listen to Dr Trump's sage advice. He has a howler of a press conference where he advises us to drink bleach, eat malaria pills, move into your sunbed and blow-torch yourself until blistered. Then you will be free of Covid-19, dear people. Satire is not possible at this advanced stage of society's malaise.'

25 April 2020
Andy Davey
Daily Telegraph

28 April 2020
Brian Adcock
Independent

Boris Johnson said the country was beginning to 'turn the tide' on coronavirus, in his first Downing Street statement since returning from hospital. 'If this virus were a physical assailant, an unexpected and invisible mugger . . . then this is the moment when we have begun together to wrestle it to the floor,' he said.

At the government's daily press briefing on coronavirus, Dominic Raab emphasised the government's commitment to 'follow the scientific evidence'. Critics had suggested that the government needed to change its strategy on issues including personal protective equipment and care homes, as it was revealed that the death toll had reached 26,000 people. But Raab argued that the government needed to stay the course, saying, 'We mustn't gamble away the sacrifices and progress we've made.'

30 April 2020
Steve Bell
Guardian

Captain Tom Moore celebrated his 100th birthday on 30 April. The war veteran had set out to raise £1,000 for NHS Charities Together by walking 100 laps of his garden – by his birthday he had raised over £32 million. For his birthday, Captain Tom was made an honorary colonel and became an honorary member of the England cricket team. The occasion was also marked with an RAF flypast and birthday greetings from the Queen and prime minister.

30 April 2020
Graeme Bandeira
Yorkshire Post

Boris Johnson and Carrie Symonds welcomed a son, Wilfred Lawrie Nicholas Johnson, on 29 April. Wilfred was reportedly Johnson's fifth child, although the prime minister has repeatedly refused to confirm how many children he has. Meanwhile, in a press conference on 30 April, Johnson announced that he would reveal a 'comprehensive plan' to restart the economy and reopen schools following the lockdown but that this plan was contingent upon the R rate – the reproduction rate of the virus – staying below one.

1 May 2020
Peter Brookes
The Times

1 May 2020
Ian Knox
Irish News

Boris Johnson's critics accused him of using the news of his son's birth to distract from the worsening coronavirus crisis. A day before the baby's arrival, Health Secretary Matt Hancock was forced to deny that the government had overlooked care homes amidst widely reported shortages of testing kits and personal protective equipment. Figures published on 28 April showed that 5,281 people had died in care homes from coronavirus, in addition to the 21,678 in hospitals. Labour MP Peter Kyle said, 'I'm convinced the loss of life in care homes could have been limited . . . They put the NHS on battle stations but they left social care as business as usual.'

GDP

Kevin Hassett, one of Donald Trump's senior economic advisers, warned that the US was entering the biggest negative drop in gross domestic product since the Great Depression as the economic fallout from coronavirus continued. More than 26 million US workers filed for unemployment in the first five weeks of lockdown – higher than the population of the country's ten most populous cities combined – with unemployment expected to rise to 20 per cent over the following two months. Hassett said that the economic forecast 'will be as bad as anything we've ever seen'. Some commentators suggested that the economy could pose a serious threat to Trump's re-election campaign.

2 May 2020
Ingram Pinn
Financial Times

STATISTICS...

Matt Hancock announced that the government had exceeded its testing target by carrying out 122,347 tests within 24 hours. However, critics claimed that, in reality, only 73,191 people had been tested and the figure had been artificially inflated by including at-home test kits that had been sent in the post but not returned. The shadow health secretary, Jon Ashworth, said, 'Far from delivering on the promise of 100,000 completed tests a day, testing numbers have now fallen three days in a row.' Meanwhile, on 5 May the UK's coronavirus death toll reached 29,427 deaths, surpassing Italy's to become the highest in Europe.

6 May 2020
Dave Brown
Independent

"I've developed an app that can track and trace medical advisors."

Professor Neil Ferguson left his post as a government scientific advisor after it was revealed that he had flouted social distancing rules. Professor Ferguson authored a report which predicted that 250,000 could die if drastic action was not taken to limit the spread of coronavirus. The *Telegraph* reported that Ferguson broke lockdown rules when his married girlfriend visited his flat. Meanwhile, the government rolled out its new 'test, track and trace' app on the Isle of Wight, designed to identify those who have been exposed to the virus.

8 May 2020
Steven Camley
Herald Scotland

It was announced that Boris Johnson would address the nation on 10 May to unveil his 'roadmap' for the lifting of lockdown. However, in the run-up to the address Johnson told the cabinet that the nation was to proceed with 'maximum caution'. In a press briefing, Dominic Raab stressed that, 'If we find in the future the R level goes back up or that people aren't following the rules, we must have the ability then to put back measures in place.'

9 May 2020
Morten Morland
The Times

Amidst reports that Boris Johnson was preparing to ease lockdown restrictions, Nicola Sturgeon warned that dropping the stay at home message could be a 'catastrophic mistake'. The first minister of Scotland said that she would prefer all four nations of the UK to make changes together but that there was potential for Scotland to go in 'different ways'. Sturgeon said she 'will not be pressured into lifting restrictions prematurely' and would 'make judgements, informed by the evidence, that are right and safe for Scotland'.

9 May 2020
Steven Camley
Herald Scotland

BACK TO WORK ...

NECROPOLITAN LINE

MIND THE GAP

14 May 2020
Dave Brown
Independent

Boris Johnson used his address to the nation on 10 May to urge people to return to work if they could not work from home. Johnson said, 'We now need to stress that anyone who can't work from home . . . should be actively encouraged to go to work.' Johnson said he was not expecting a 'sudden big flood' of people returning to work but Labour Leader Keir Starmer criticised the prime minister for 'effectively telling millions of people to go back to work tomorrow'. The next day, images emerged of London underground trains packed with commuters.

The prime minister's speech on 10 May outlined the first steps to allow the nation to emerge from lockdown. Boris Johnson announced that people were now allowed to leave their homes more than once a day, as well as play some sports and meet other people in public parks, provided they maintained social distancing. He also confirmed that schools in England would begin to reopen from June and that restaurants could begin to reopen from July. However, many criticised the government's new 'stay alert' policy for being vague and confusing – Keir Starmer said that the guidance 'just isn't clear enough'.

17 May 2020
Chris Riddell
Observer

PROTECTIVE RING SUPPLIES ARE AT RECORD LEVELS!

19 May 2020
Steve Bell
Guardian

Speaking at a Downing Street press conference, Health Secretary Matt Hancock said that he had 'tried to put a protective ring around our care homes' from the beginning of the pandemic, despite complaints of a lack of testing and personal protective equipment. Hancock announced new measures to test every care home resident and staff member for the virus and to instruct local authorities – which said they faced a shortfall of £3.5 billion in their social care budget – to conduct daily reviews of care homes. The most recent figures showed that there had been 8,312 deaths in care homes from coronavirus.

After touting the effectiveness of hydroxychloroquine in April, Donald Trump announced that he had been taking a daily dose of the drug himself to ward off coronavirus. Not only is there no evidence that the anti-malarial drug helps to prevent the virus, some studies suggest it may increase the risk of death. The US Food and Drug Administration said that hydroxychloroquine has 'not been shown to be safe' and, in some studies, had been shown to cause heart failure, suicidal thoughts and liver disease. President Trump said, 'I get a lot of tremendously positive news on the hydroxy . . . What do you have to lose?'

19 May 2020
Dave Brown
Independent

THE POINT MAN

President Trump repeatedly accused China of concealing evidence and allowing coronavirus to spread, tweeting 'it was the "incompetence of China", and nothing else, that did this mass Worldwide killing!' Trump also said that President Obama had 'made a decision on testing that turned out to be very detrimental' even though scientists said that they did not know what Trump was referring to. And he blamed the World Health Organisation for 'severely mismanaging' the crisis and for being too 'China-centric'. The administration even blamed the American people for having 'a significantly disproportionate burden of comorbidities . . . [including] obesity, hypertension, diabetes'.

20 May 2020
Kevin Kallaugher
Economist

Boris Johnson revealed that foreign NHS staff would have to continue to pay large fees to use the health service despite admitting that foreign carers had 'frankly, saved my life'. The Labour Party called for the government to scrap the policy, but the prime minister claimed that the NHS would be short of funds without it. Under the policy, a family of four on a five-year work permit would have had to pay up to £8,000 to use NHS services. Two days later, Johnson announced that he had reversed his decision and that the fees would be axed as soon as possible. Keir Starmer responded that it was the right decision as 'We cannot clap our carers one day and then charge them to use our NHS the next.'

22 May 2020
Steve Bell
Guardian

22 May 2020
Ben Jennings
i

Britons flocked to the beaches on 20 May as the UK saw the hottest day of the year so far. Lockdown restrictions had been eased only ten days earlier, giving people the chance to drive to beauty spots for 'unlimited exercise'. Thousands of people gathered on beaches in Brighton, Bournemouth and Blackpool with some appearing to shun social distancing advice, raising concerns about a second wave of infections. One local man said, 'It's madness, it's like everyone's forgotten about coronavirus.'

The prime minister's chief adviser, Dominic Cummings, faced calls to resign after he breached lockdown rules by travelling to Durham from his home in London whilst showing symptoms of coronavirus. At the time government guidance was that 'You should not be visiting family members who do not live in your home.' Cummings said he had travelled north to stay with his parents as he was worried that he and his wife would not be able to care for their son if their condition worsened. Boris Johnson backed Cummings, saying he had 'acted responsibly, legally and with integrity', but scientists protested that defending Cummings undermined efforts to curb the spread of the virus.

25 May 2020
Brian Adcock
Independent

On 25 May an unarmed black man, George Floyd, died in police custody after a white police officer knelt on his neck for eight minutes as he was arrested. A video later emerged of Floyd pleading 'I can't breathe' as the police officer cut off his air supply. Floyd's death sparked Black Lives Matter protests across the world. Although the majority of US demonstrations were peaceful, when some turned violent President Trump threatened to send in the military to 'restore safety and security in America'. The cartoon references Joe Rosenthal's photograph of US marines raising the American flag on Iwo Jima in February 1945.

3 June 2020
Peter Brookes
The Times

Belltoons.co.uk

I'M TAKING BACK CONTROL!

©Steve Bell 2020-4·6-4510-

Boris Johnson announced that he had decided to 'take back control' of the coronavirus response, leading some to question who had been leading the government response before. The prime minister's comment came after a turbulent couple of weeks in which his chief aide was accused of breaking lockdown restrictions and the test and trace scheme suffered major technical setbacks. Keir Starmer said that Johnson needed to 'get a grip' of the coronavirus crisis and accused Johnson of 'winging it'.

4 June 2020
Steve Bell
Guardian

"LAW AND ORDER"

As protests grew following the death of George Floyd, Donald Trump ordered security forces to break up a peaceful protest outside the White House using tear gas and rubber bullets. This was to enable the president to walk across the park to a boarded-up church, holding a Bible aloft for a photo opportunity. *CNN* called the move a 'made-for-TV embrace of authoritarianism's imagery . . . a moment of vanity and bravado'. The Right Reverend Mariann Budde commented, 'He was using our church as the backdrop and the Bible as a prop in ways that I found to be deeply offensive.'

5 June 2020
Ingram Pinn
Financial Times

The protests following the death of George Floyd became the worst civil unrest in America since the assassination of Martin Luther King Jr. In a leaked call with state governors, the president stressed the need to 'dominate' the protestors and demanded governors call in the National Guard. Later, combat soldiers were moved within reach of Washington and Trump tweeted that any protestor who breached the White House fence would be met with 'vicious dogs' and 'ominous weapons'. It was also revealed that Trump had been taken to a security bunker for safety. The president denied these reports – he had only gone to the bunker for the purposes of 'inspection', he said.

6 June 2020
Chris Riddell
Guardian

During an anti-racism demonstration in Bristol a statue of a 17th-century slave trader was torn down and thrown into the harbour, a move Boris Johnson denounced as 'a criminal act'. According to the cartoonist, 'I remembered how Boris had gone off on holiday at a vital time. I recalled the lack of PPE for our brave NHS staff. How the elderly were discharged from hospital and sent back to their care homes without a Covid test. How the government lied to hit their 100,000 tests a day target . . . How Boris had defended Dominic Cummings . . . as my sadness, frustration and anger grew, I suddenly thought to myself, "It's not the Statue of Edward Colston that should have been thrown into the sea!"'

9 June 2020
Mal Humphreys
Western Mail

In response to President Trump's threats against Black Lives Matter protesters, over 280 former US diplomats and military leaders signed a letter condemning Trump's plans to call in the military, criticising the 'misuse of the military for political purposes'. Across the pond, Boris Johnson acknowledged that there was 'much more to do' to fight racism but also said that the protests had been 'subverted by thuggery' and those who broke the rules would face 'the full force of the law'. Meanwhile, HBO removed the film *Gone with the Wind* from its streaming library; the film had long been criticised for romanticising slavery and the Civil War-era American South.

10 June 2020
Dave Brown
Independent

With the death toll from coronavirus reaching 40,000, the government faced growing questions over the UK's response to the pandemic. A Downing Street spokesman defended the government's reaction saying, 'This is an unprecedented global pandemic and we have taken the right steps at the right time to combat it.' However, critics said that the government had been slow to announce a lockdown, slow to implement routine testing, slow to develop a test and trace policy, slow to acquire the necessary personal protective equipment and slow to recognise the crisis in care homes.

10 June 2020
Peter Brookes
The Times

HIS DARKEST HOUR

Protestors daubed a statue of Winston Churchill with the words 'was a racist' during a Black Lives Matter demonstration. In anticipation of further protests, the statue in Parliament Square was boxed up to prevent further damage, along with other key statues such as the Cenotaph war memorial and a statue of Nelson Mandela. Boris Johnson said that the vandalism was 'absurd and shameful' and, whilst Churchill expressed views that are now considered unacceptable, 'We cannot pretend to have a different history.'

12 June 2020
Paul Thomas
Daily Mail

15 June 2020
Patrick Blower
Daily Telegraph

Shops in England began to reopen in June after a three-month lockdown. Consumers flocked to stores, with the Birmingham Primark opening at 7:30am to accommodate the hundreds of people queuing outside and the IKEA store in Warrington seeing a queue of 1,000 people arriving from 5:40am. Strict safety measures, including plastic screens at the tills and floor markings, were installed in most stores in order to keep shoppers two metres apart. Other measures included asking customers not to touch goods they didn't intend to buy, toilet and fitting-room closures and installation of hand-sanitiser stations.

Footballer Marcus Rashford criticised the government after ministers said they would not continue to provide free school meals to children who qualify for them during the summer holidays. In an emotional letter to MPs, Rashford asked, 'Political affiliations aside, can we not all agree that no child should be going to bed hungry?' A day later, the government reversed its decision, with Boris Johnson praising Rashford's 'contribution to the debate around poverty'.

17 June 2020
Brian Adcock
Independent

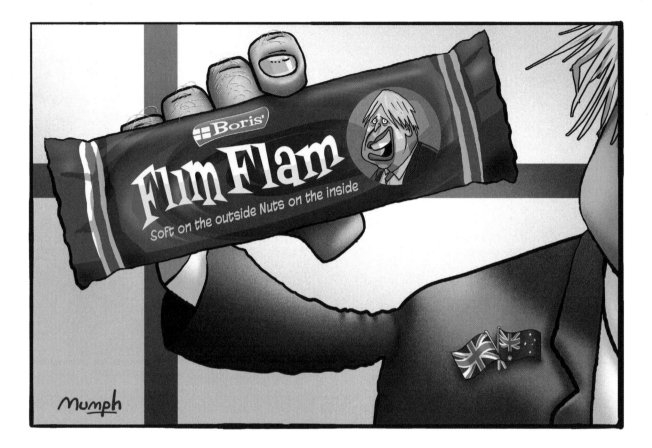

Boris Johnson welcomed post-Brexit trade talks between the UK and Australia as a chance to bring the two countries closer together. The prime minister pointed out that one of the most significant benefits would be that the two countries could now exchange their most famous biscuit products. 'How long can the British people be deprived of the opportunity to have Tim Tams at a reasonable price?' the prime minister asked. According to the cartoonist, Johnson 'prattled on in a most bizarre way about Marmite, Vegemite and Penguins. Next came the sound of rustling polythene as he tried to promote the virtues of Tim Tams . . . I was left scratching my head, wondering what exactly I'd listened to.'

17 June 2020
Mal Humphreys
Western Mail

The prime minister announced that the Department for International Development (DfID) was to be merged into the Foreign and Commonwealth Office after 20 years of independence. Decisions about foreign aid would now be made by the foreign secretary, thereby linking the UK's aid spending to its political interests. 'For too long, frankly, UK overseas aid has been treated like a giant cashpoint in the sky,' Johnson said. However, three former prime ministers, David Cameron, Gordon Brown and Tony Blair, all criticised the move. According to the cartoonist, 'Boris Johnson took the opportunity, while everybody was concentrating on the deadly Covid-19 fiasco, to feed some red meat to his backbench right-wing nutjobs'.

18 June 2020
Andy Davey
Daily Telegraph

Boris Johnson declared that pubs, restaurants and hairdressers would be able to reopen from 4 July. He also announced that the two-metre rule would be changed to 'one-metre-plus', meaning that people should stay at least one metre apart when two metres was not possible. However, the UK's scientific advisers warned that a one-metre distance carries up to ten times the risk compared to being two metres apart. According to Schrank, 'Most politicians enjoy appearing in cartoons ... Which kind of defeats the purpose, from our perspective. Occasionally an opportunity arises to show them as ineffectual and isolated ... Politicians don't enjoy that.'

22 June 2020
Peter Schrank
The Times

There were calls for an inquiry after Robert Jenrick, the secretary of state for housing, allegedly aided a billionaire property developer to avoid £40 million in local council charges. Former media tycoon Richard Desmond, a significant donor to the Conservative Party, had 24 hours to have the development approved before he incurred millions in community charges. Jenrick overruled local officials to approve the development on time. The development is in the most deprived borough of London, Tower Hamlets, whose council uses the charge to invest in poorer communities. After being challenged on the decision, Jenrick admitted that it had been unlawful.

23 June 2020
Morten Morland
The Times

26 June 2020
Christian Adams
Evening Standard

Labour leader Sir Keir Starmer fired shadow cabinet minister Rebecca Long Bailey after she shared an article on Twitter that many alleged contained an antisemitic conspiracy theory. The shadow education secretary protested that she had not intended to support all aspects of the article. The Labour Party has faced claims of antisemitism since 2016 but Starmer declared his intention to deal with antisemitism 'robustly and swiftly' when he took over as Labour leader. Some of Long Bailey's allies questioned whether Sir Keir was looking for an excuse to marginalise the left of the party.

Sir Mark Sedwill, the UK's most senior civil servant, stepped down from his role after reports that he had been sidelined by the prime minister and his senior aide, Dominic Cummings. The civil servants' union, the FDA, commented that Sir Mark had been undermined in a 'cowardly' way. Dominic Cummings has long called for a shake-up of the civil service and a number of top civil servants had left their posts following the Conservatives' election victory.

30 June 2020
Brian Adcock
Independent

1 July 2020
Patrick Blower
Daily Telegraph

On 29 June it was announced that the UK's first local lockdown would be implemented in Leicester. The city's infection rate was 135 cases per 100,000 people, three times that of the next highest city, and accounted for 10 per cent of all confirmed cases in the previous week. All non-essential shops and schools in Leicester were closed and people were told to avoid travelling in and out of the city. The following day, Boris Johnson announced an 'ambitious' economic recovery plan worth £5 billion to build homes and infrastructure. The prime minister promised to 'build, build, build' to compensate for the economic shock of coronavirus.

THE SECOND WAVE

From 4 July pubs in England were allowed to reopen. In a press conference, Boris Johnson urged customers to act sensibly, warning 'we are not out of the woods yet'. However, some argued that the government's plea to act sensibly did not fit with regulations that allowed pubs to start serving alcohol from 6am on a Saturday. The Treasury even posted a tweet encouraging people to 'grab a drink and raise a glass', though it was later deleted. Commentators expressed concern that social drinking and drunken behaviour could lead to a second wave of the virus.

3 July 2020
Dave Brown
Independent

6 July 2020
Brian Adcock
Independent

Saturday 4 July became known as 'Super Saturday' as pubs, bars, cafés and restaurants opened for the first time in three months. Hundreds of thousands of people visited bars over the weekend, raising concerns that many were not observing social distancing. Images emerged of the streets in Soho, central London, packed with revellers until the early hours of Sunday morning – one social media user described the scenes as a coronavirus 'petri dish'. Some pubs in Nottingham and Leicestershire also had to close due to crowding. Chairman of the Police Federation John Apter commented, 'What was crystal clear is that drunk people can't/won't socially distance.'

Rishi Sunak threw a lifeline to Britain's struggling theatres, music venues, cinema, galleries and museums, offering £1.57 billion in loans and grants. Unable to stage live performances, some theatres and venues had already announced redundancies and closures. Lord Andrew Lloyd-Webber commented that the 'news is truly welcome at a time when so many theatres, orchestras, entertainment venues and other arts organisations face such a bleak future'.

6 July 2020
Graeme Bandeira
Yorkshire Post

Boris Johnson drew criticism from health officials, unions and MPs after he implied that care homes were to blame for the huge death toll amongst the elderly. 'We discovered too many care homes didn't really follow the procedures in the way that they could have' the prime minister commented, although he did admit that the government needed to ensure proper organisation and funding for care homes. Nadra Ahmed, chair of the National Care Association, said Johnson's comments were 'a huge slap in the face'. It had recently been revealed that over 20,000 care home residents had died with coronavirus, with one in five residents and 7 per cent of staff infected.

7 July 2020
Christian Adams
Evening Standard

'To get customers back into restaurants, cafés and pubs, and protect the 1.8 million people who work in them, I can announce today that, for the month of August, we will give everyone in the country an "Eat Out to Help Out" discount', Chancellor Rishi Sunak announced. The scheme offered diners a discount of up to £10 per person from Monday to Wednesday, and was designed to support the hospitality industry during the pandemic. Seeking to reassure the public that it was safe to dine out, Sunak said, 'I know people are cautious about going out. But we wouldn't have lifted the restrictions if we didn't think we could do so safely.'

9 July 2020
Dave Brown
Independent

The US Supreme Court ruled that New York prosecutors investigating Donald Trump could have access to his financial records, a decision the president described as a 'witch-hunt'. Trump had repeatedly come under fire for refusing to share his tax returns, justifying this by claiming that he had total immunity while in office. However, the court ruled that the tax records should be handed over as part of an investigation into hush payments, including one to porn-star Stormy Daniels. Meanwhile, Trump held his Independence Day address at Mount Rushmore, using the opportunity to attack the left and protestors against racial injustice.

10 July 2020
Steve Bell
Guardian

Boris Johnson backed former cabinet minister Chris Grayling for the post of chair of the Intelligence and Security Committee (ISC), although his appointment was delayed while the government searched for other nominees to the committee who would be willing to support him. Grayling was one of five Conservative MPs to join the nine-person committee, which oversees MI6, MI5 and GCHQ. The committee had the power to release or delay the report into Russian interference in UK politics, which Johnson was accused of stifling before the December election. The former chair of the ISC, Dominic Grieve, called on the committee to release the report as soon as possible.

11 July 2020
Chris Riddell
Observer

12 July 2020
Ben Jennings
Guardian

Donald Trump was seen wearing a mask in public for the first time, having previously stated that he would never wear one. 'Wearing a face mask as I greet presidents, prime ministers, dictators, kings, queens – I just don't see it', Trump said. However, Trump changed his tune after the US recorded 66,528 coronavirus cases in a single day on 11 July, a new daily record. 'I'm all for masks', Trump commented in an interview with Fox, adding that he believed wearing a mask made him look like the Lone Ranger. At the time, America had recorded almost 135,000 coronavirus deaths.

FACE MASK POLICY

Blower 14.7.20

The government announced that it would be mandatory to wear face masks in shops in England from 24 July, in response to mounting evidence that masks help to prevent transmission of coronavirus. However, in a BBC interview, senior minister Michael Gove said that he did not think masks should be compulsory. Rishi Sunak was criticised for posing without a face covering when serving food in Wagamama's, while Justice Secretary Robert Buckland said face masks should be 'mandatory perhaps'. Labour's Jonathan Ashworth said the government response had been 'slow and muddled again'.

14 July 2020
Patrick Blower
Daily Telegraph

Foreign Secretary Dominic Raab, who has a black belt in karate, revealed that the UK would suspend its extradition treaty with Hong Kong 'immediately and indefinitely', after the Chinese government imposed a new security law on the territory. The new law gave Beijing extensive control over Hong Kong and introduces new crimes, including making it illegal to incite 'hatred' of the Chinese government. Such crimes carry severe penalties. New provisions also gave the Chinese government jurisdiction over certain legal cases and allowed those trials to be held in secret and without a jury. The extradition treaty had meant that if someone in the UK had been accused of a crime in Hong Kong, British authorities would have had to hand them over to face justice – and vice versa.

21 July 2020
Patrick Blower
Daily Telegraph

The long-awaited report into Russian interference was finally published in July, concluding that Downing Street 'threw a blanket' over Russian meddling in UK politics. The report drew a picture of 'a government that didn't want to know, and of spooks who were too timid to ask', according to the *Guardian*. 'After this cartoon was published it was pointed out to me that I was in danger of mixing up my cuddly bear metaphors,' says Schrank. 'Xi Jinping of China was compared to Winnie the Pooh by Chinese bloggers, and he is rather sensitive about it . . . Perhaps I should have referred to Paddington Bear instead.'

22 July 2020
Peter Schrank
The Times

In a visit to Orkney, Boris Johnson claimed that the coronavirus response had demonstrated the 'sheer might' of the Union. In response, Nicola Sturgeon criticised the prime minister for using coronavirus as a 'political weapon'. The disagreement came as polls showed an increase in support for Scottish independence after the Scottish government's more cautious response to the pandemic. As he arrived in Scotland, Johnson was greeted by a small protest waving signs that said 'Hands off Scotland' and 'Our Scotland, our future'.

24 July 2020
Steve Bell
Guardian

A SPOONLESS of SUGAR ...

Boris Johnson introduced an initiative to help the nation lose weight, including a 12-week plan to develop healthier eating habits and be more active. It was revealed after scientists warned that obesity is 'the single most important modifiable risk factor' in tackling coronavirus. The campaign, called Better Health was designed to reverse bad dietary and exercise habits that people had lapsed into during lockdown. It particularly focused on people of black and Asian backgrounds who have suffered disproportionately high death rates. NHS weight loss services were expected to be expanded and GPs were encouraged to prescribe cycling.

26 July 2020
Nicola Jennings
Guardian

Britons travelling back to the UK from Spain would have to quarantine on return, the government announced. Chief Medical Officer Chris Whitty said 'doing nothing isn't an option' after a surge in cases on the continent. Spain had recently recorded 922 infections in a day and officials were tracking more than 280 outbreaks across the country. Other European countries, including France, Germany and Belgium, all reported steep rises in cases. Earlier in the month, the government had published a list of 73 countries which would be exempt from quarantine rules. Controversially, Portugal was not among them, a decision Lisbon called 'absurd'.

29 July 2020
Patrick Blower
Daily Telegraph

A new statue, entitled 'The End', was unveiled on the Fourth Plinth in Trafalgar Square depicting a melting swirl of ice cream, complete with a cherry. The artist, Heather Phillipson, said the sculpture represented the 'idea of something being on the verge of collapse'. Meanwhile, the *Evening Standard* reported that Boris Johnson was 'extremely concerned' about a second wave of coronavirus within the next two weeks, following a surge in cases across Europe. The government had warned that a second wave was possible in winter, but now feared it would arrive sooner.

30 July 2020
Christian Adams
Evening Standard

According to Baron, 'I was thinking of how coronavirus has reshaped and reconfigured so many different aspects of our lives. And I wanted this cartoon to be a bit positive. The virus has made a hole in the fabric of our world, but things are starting to come back. People are going to fly a bit less and hopefully care about the environment a bit more . . . In the beginning of the pandemic, I was feeling fairly useless: why wasn't I doing something useful like working as a nurse? But my drawings about Covid-19 have got the most response I've ever had and that has felt really good.'

31 July 2020
Ella Baron
Observer

'Resurgent coronavirus was "bubbling up" in up to 30 areas across Britain, Boris Johnson warned', writes Davey. 'He had already imposed a new lockdown on the first of them, Leicester. Others began to spring up in the north. He had previously alluded to localised responses to outbreaks as like playing "whack-a-mole", although in that game, only one mole pops up at a time. He realised he might need a sledgehammer to solve the problem.'

1 August 2020
Andy Davey
Daily Telegraph

A study conducted by University College London suggested that public trust in the government's handling of coronavirus had been significantly damaged by Dominic Cummings' trip to Durham in March. The report coincided with several witness reports that Cummings was also in Durham in April. The study showed a clear drop in confidence in the government starting on 22 May, after the story broke, continuing to fall in the following days. Cummings' actions also had an impact on the public's willingness to follow the lockdown guidelines, according to researchers.

9 August 2020
Chris Riddell
Observer

A Home Office source denounced Ben and Jerry's as 'overpriced junk food' after the ice cream brand took to Twitter to criticise Priti Patel's migrant policy. In a series of tweets, the company criticised Patel's 'lack of humanity' and commented, 'People cannot be illegal.' The government had earlier said that the UK must reconsider asylum laws to deter people from crossing the Channel. Patel had described the number of boats making the crossing as 'appalling and unacceptably high'.

12 August 2020
Graeme Bandeira
Yorkshire Post

The prime minister warned that there was a 'long, long way to go' before the economy would improve. New figures showed that, between April and June, the number of people in work fell by 220,000 – the largest drop in over a decade. Analysts said that unemployment was set to worsen as the furlough scheme was wound down, warning of a looming 'cliff-edge'. Meanwhile, data showed that the economy had contracted by 20.4 per cent in the second quarter of 2020. However, Boris Johnson said that he had 'absolutely no doubt' that government schemes would help the economy to become 'stronger than ever before'.

12 August 2020
Brian Adcock
Independent

RUNNING MATE...

US presidential nominee Joe Biden selected Kamala Harris as his running mate, making the senator from California the first black and Asian American woman to run on a major party's presidential ticket. According to a Reuters and Ipsos poll, Harris is even more popular than Biden among women, young voters and some Republicans. 60 per cent of women said they had a favourable view of Harris, compared to 53 per cent who said the same about Biden.

13 August 2020
Morten Morland
The Times

Transport Secretary Grant Shapps announced that a 14-day quarantine would be imposed on travellers returning from France, after the country saw a 66 per cent rise in coronavirus cases. The announcement triggered chaos as many of the estimated 160,000 British tourists in France tried to return before quarantine measures came into force. Eurotunnel bosses said a total of 22 extra departures were scheduled, carrying more than 30,000 passengers in 11,600 vehicles. The race to book flights saw air fares soar to six times their normal price.

15 August 2020
Brian Adcock
Independent

At the same time as thousands of British tourists were seeking to make it home from France to avoid the quarantine deadline, record numbers of migrants were also crossing the Dover strait. Conservative MPs labelled the crossings an 'invasion', with Home Secretary Priti Patel stepping up plans to send in Royal Navy warships to intercept migrants and appointing a new 'clandestine Channel threat commander'. One Ministry of Defence official responded, 'It's beyond absurd to think that we should be deploying multimillion-pound ships and elite soldiers to deal with desperate people barely staying afloat on rubber dinghies.'

15 August 2020
Morten Morland
The Times

"IT'S A NEW ALGORITHM TO CALCULATE HOW LONG BEFORE YOU LOSE YOUR JOB, MINISTER"

After school exams were cancelled due to coronavirus, grades were awarded based on teacher-predicted grades and class rankings, with an algorithm used to standardise the results. On results day 36 per cent of A-Level grades were lower than teachers predicted. One student said that she was 'ruined' after her ABB predictions were downgraded to DDD. Education Secretary Gavin Williamson faced numerous calls to resign over the government's handling of the results. *The Times* reported that Sir Jon Coles, a former director general at the Department for Education, had warned Williamson in July that the algorithm would only be 75 per cent accurate, putting hundreds of thousands of students at risk.

19 August 2020
Paul Thomas
Daily Mail

After a government U-turn, it was announced that A-Level and GSCE grades would be based on teacher recommendations only. Critics claimed that the algorithm that had originally been used to standardise results was unlawful as it had unfairly privileged private schools with smaller classes, whilst penalising more disadvantaged and diverse state schools. Many university places had already been awarded based on the algorithm-predicted results, causing admissions chaos. According to the cartoonist, 'Doing a cartoon about A-Level results can feel a bit like an annual ritual, and sometimes it's difficult to find inspiration. Not so this year. Which proves once again that bad news, and bad governments, are good news for cartoonists.'

19 August 2020
Peter Schrank
The Times

The DRIVERLESS CAR

BURKE 2020

It was revealed that partially self-driving cars could be on British roads as early as 2021, according to proposals being considered by the government. Car manufacturers are expected to roll out technology that would enable cars to keep within lanes and avoid collisions without any driver assistance. This technology could even be used at speeds up to 70 miles per hour. The transport minister, Rachel Maclean, said, 'Automated technology could make driving safer, smoother and easier for motorists, and the UK should be the first country to see these benefits.'

23 August 2020
Chris Burke
The Times

Boris Johnson left ministers in charge of an exam crisis, a recession and the coronavirus pandemic while he went on a camping holiday in Scotland with his partner and baby son. Twitter users voiced their disapproval of the prime minister's absence using the hashtag #WheresBoris. Meanwhile, even though coronavirus cases had been increasing for several weeks, hospital admissions and deaths related to Covid-19 were at record lows in the UK. In the week ending 21 August, British hospitals admitted an average of just over 84 people a day with Covid-19 – less than at any stage during the pandemic.

24 August 2020
Ben Jennings
Guardian

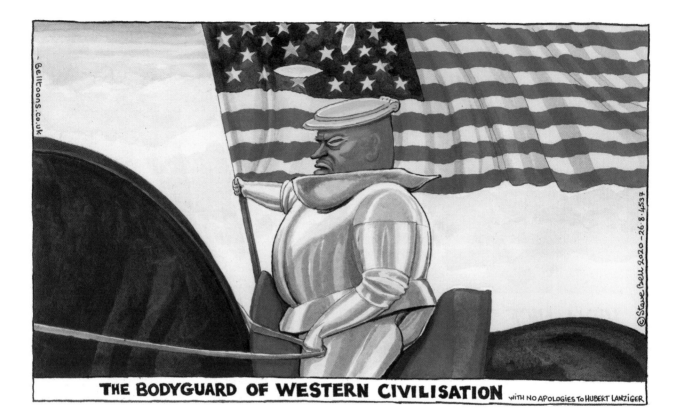

THE BODYGUARD OF WESTERN CIVILISATION WITH NO APOLOGIES TO HUBERT LANZIGER

In the US, the Republican National Convention was opened by Charlie Kirk, a conservative youth activist, who called President Trump 'the bodyguard of western civilization'. He went on to say, 'Trump was elected to protect our families from the vengeful mob that seeks to destroy our way of life, our neighbourhoods, schools, churches and values.' At the convention, Trump was officially named the Republican Party nominee for the 2020 election. Bell based this cartoon on a Nazi propaganda painting by Hubert Lanzinger, which showed Hitler as a noble warrior, gazing towards a better future for Germany, with the Nazi flag flying behind him.

26 August 2020
Steve Bell
Guardian

Following reports that 'Rule, Britannia!' and 'Land of Hope and Glory' would not be played at the Proms due to references to colonialism and slavery in the lyrics, the BBC confirmed that the songs would be performed but not sung. A report in the *Sunday Times* suggested that Proms conductor, Dalia Stasevska, believes it is time 'to bring change' – a view that attracted much criticism. Boris Johnson responded, 'I think it's time we stopped our cringing embarrassment about our history . . . and we stopped this general fight of self-recrimination and wetness.'

27 August 2020
Dave Brown
Independent

WAKE UP AND SMELL THE ...

COALITION 2010

28 August 2020
Dave Brown
Independent

Ed Davey was elected the new leader of the Liberal Democrats after beating his rival, Layla Moran, by 42,756 votes to 24,564. Davey urged his party to 'wake up and smell the coffee' after three poor election results. In his acceptance speech, Davey said, 'My job, as from today, is to rebuild the Lib Dems to national relevance . . . voters don't believe we are on the side of people like them.' Davey was a cabinet minister in the coalition government but lost his seat after the Lib Dems' crushing defeat in the 2015 election. He won his seat back in 2017.

At least one member of the Trump family spoke on each evening of the Republican National Convention, highlighting the extent to which President Trump and his family have become a political brand. Trump's wife, Melania, all four of his adult children, Don Jr., Eric, Ivanka and Tiffany, as well as his daughter-in-law, Lara Trump, and Trump Jr.'s partner, Kimberley Guilfoyle, all spoke at the convention. In his bombastic speech, Donald Trump Jr. referred to the Democratic nominee, Joe Biden, as 'Beijing Biden' and said that, 'the radical left are also now coming for our freedom of speech and want to bully us into submission.'

30 August 2020
Chris Riddell
Observer

Newspapers reported that Chancellor Rishi Sunak was drawing up plans to raise taxes in order to recover the £26.7 billion borrowed to deal with the economic fallout of coronavirus. It was suggested that pension tax relief could be cut, capital gains tax increased and corporation tax adjusted from 19 per cent to 24 per cent, in addition to cuts to foreign aid. The reports came at the same time as the news that UK public sector debt had hit more than £2 trillion for the first time ever, meaning that public debt was higher than the UK's gross domestic product.

31 August 2020
Morten Morland
The Times